T0305373

The North Sea System for Petroleum Production

The North Sea System for Petroleum Production

State Intervention on the British and Norwegian Continental Shelves

Brent F. Nelsen

Jane Fishburne Hipp Professor of Politics and International Affairs, Furman University, USA

Tina Soliman Hunter

Professor of Energy and Natural Resources Law, and Director of the Centre for Energy Resources Innovation and Transformation (CENRIT), Macquarie University, Australia

 Edward Elgar
PUBLISHING

Cheltenham, UK • Northampton, MA, USA

Published by
Edward Elgar Publishing Limited
The Lypiatts
15 Lansdown Road
Cheltenham
Glos GL50 2JA
UK

Edward Elgar Publishing, Inc.
William Pratt House
9 Dewey Court
Northampton
Massachusetts 01060
USA

A catalogue record for this book
is available from the British Library

Library of Congress Control Number: 2023952686

This book is available electronically in the **Elgar**online
Law subject collection
http://dx.doi.org/10.4337/9781839102509

ISBN 978 1 83910 249 3 (cased)
ISBN 978 1 83910 250 9 (eBook)

Printed and bound by CPI Group (UK) Ltd, Croydon, CR0 4YY

In Memory of Professor Martin Sæter,
Who gave me the freedom to pursue my policy passion.
Brent F. Nelsen

To Professor dr juris Ernst Nordveit,
Who sparked my interest, fueled my imagination, and was
always there as I followed my dreams.
Tina Soliman Hunter

Contents

Tables

Figures

Preface

It's all Tina's fault! I (Brent) wrote my dissertation and published a book on North Sea oil and gas policy in the early 1990s (*The State Offshore*) and then moved on to other topics. But I decided to dip my toe back in the water when a Furman colleague and good friend of mine, Bill Ranson, a geologist by discipline, suggested we team up to lead a 'May Experience' ('MayX' in Furman speak) to the Nordic regions. I had led several trips to Scandinavia to study social policy, but here was a colleague suggesting we could take students to study energy policy. The result was a MayX to Iceland, Scotland, and Norway with 25 students in 2018 to study 'Nordic Energy and Energy Policy'. To prepare for the course, I dusted off my old copy of *The State Offshore* and assigned parts to my students to read. To my surprise, I remembered how much I used to like this stuff!

This is where Tina comes in. I knew Tina only by her publications, but decided to email her at the University of Aberdeen to see if she would be willing to speak to my students and update them on happenings on the continental shelf since 1991 (yes, that is a long time!). To my surprise, she agreed! And when our group of 27 arrived, we were greeted by the most enthusiastic, knowledgeable, and simply fun academic we met the whole month. Tina gave a fantastic lecture, but more important, she took the students seriously. I was drawn to her. After the lecture, as we walked across campus to the waiting coach, Tina explained to me how my ancient book was still required reading for students interested in offshore policy. She asked if I had ever considered updating it. The short answer was no, but in a moment of weakness, I suggested that I might if she would agree to co-author it with me. It took her a New York second to agree. And the book was launched.

There were obstacles, as there are with every major endeavour. The COVID-19 pandemic intervened. Personal illnesses, moves to different hemi-spheres, administrative tasks, prior projects, teaching – all conspired against us. But finally, after more emails, WhatsApp messages, and transcontinental/hemispheric Zoom calls than we can count, we finished the project. It still took the talents and patience of Ben Booth and Elizabeth Ruck, both at Edward Elgar Publishing, to get the book into print. But somehow it all came together.

This book seeks to explain why two countries with similar (by global standards) political systems producing oil and gas from the same geographic region varied their approaches to state intervention in the petroleum industry over time. Sometimes the two countries adopted the same strategy; other times they diverged dramatically. In the 1960s, before petroleum had been discovered offshore, both the British and Norwegian states adopted a 'minimal intervention' approach that gave great latitude to international oil companies with the knowledge and experience to drill in risky waters. The states had to attract foreign investment. But while they were competitors for exploration dollars, they also looked to each other for policy ideas. Thus, the initial offshore systems they established looked quite similar. After the companies struck huge petroleum fields, however, both states moved away from minimal intervention and adopted a 'participatory intervention' model that tightly regulated the offshore activities, but also demanded that the private companies allow the states, through newly created state oil companies, to participate as part owners of offshore joint ventures. The early 1980s saw another big shift as British and Norwegian state intervention policies diverged dramatically. Britain dismantled its offshore participation infrastructure and exited the North Sea as an owner. In place of participation, the state adopted a 'regulatory intervention' strategy. Meanwhile, Norway tinkered a bit with its participation on the continental shelf but remained committed to participatory intervention.

Since the 1990s, the North Sea has matured as a petroleum sector. The big fields have been producing for a long time; new fields are smaller and more difficult to exploit. The result has been a reconvergence of strategy as Britain and Norway have sought to maximize the recovery of hydrocarbons instead of leaving harder-to-produce deposits in the ground. Both states have tightened their regulatory control of offshore activities, but the Norwegians have not completely turned away from their offshore participation model. So, here is the puzzle: Why has intervention strategy varied over time and between these two countries?

The policy process in any liberal democracy is extremely complex. There is no one factor that explains variation in policy. System pressures emanating from big power competition, oil market players, economic conditions, the capacity of bureaucracies to handle information, and regulatory enforcement play a big role – so too do political parties and interest groups. Perhaps most interesting to us is how political culture can influence government actors to prefer some policy solutions over others. The British, while generally favorable to market solutions to policy problems, do have a strong Fabian influence that resurfaces now and then to encourage deeper state involvement in the economy. Norway, on the other hand, has been very comfortable with public ownership of important industries and strong state influence over private enterprise since its independence in 1905. We do not promise a grand theory to explain exactly how each of these factors interact with the others. But we do describe how these factors influence the bargaining relationships between the relevant actors leading to a narrowing of policy options for decision makers. We explain the general direction of policy, but it is beyond our scope to explain more. We leave that to the economists.

In the mid-2020s, we are seeing the beginnings of a new phase of the North Sea system. The production of oil and gas continues, but petroleum increasingly shares the sea with green energy activities – wind farms, carbon capture, and soon, hydrogen production. The new and the old are intertwining as they use some of the same offshore infrastructure to produce and reduce carbon emissions at the same time. Petroleum production could be completely shut down in the North Sea in the next five years. But that is highly unlikely, despite the pressure on politicians from environmental groups and others. No, the offshore dance is likely to continue for a generation or more before renewable energy and carbon capture become the only offshore activities left. When the petroleum is gone or scorned, the North Sea will continue to produce energy; it just won't produce carbon. But it will remain an amazing – and lucrative – resource for the countries privileged to border it.

Acknowledgments

Every book is a community project. This one is no exception. We, of course, take responsibility for any errors.

I (Brent) stand on the broad shoulders of the colleagues and friends I worked with in the petroleum group at the Norwegian Institute of International Affairs (NUPI) in the late 1980s. Martin Sæter was the *éminence gris* of our little band of young (very young) scholars with a deep interest in Norway's new offshore industry. Magne Holter, Janne Haaland Matláry, and Ole Gunnar Austvik have all gone on to great things in their fields, but they left a deep mark on me as a graduate student in search of a dissertation. My Furman colleagues Bill Ranson, Jim Guth, and Glen Halva-Neubauer have supported me in this project and humored me when I rambled too long about semi-submersible rigs. Students on the Nordic Energy trip, who had to read my first North Sea book, earnestly encouraged me to take up the challenge of a second. Those included Emily Bolvig, Hunter Dixon, Jackson Ferrell, Grace Gwynn, Catherine Hayward, C. J. Lane, and Jackson Robinson. Joshua Woodfin, my summer 2022 research fellow, read and organized articles, constructed figures, and read through the early chapters. He was indispensable as a researcher and became a good friend. Another student, Michael Peeler, also proved his weight in gold by finding and fixing several data errors that were hampering our construction of some of the graphs. My warmest thanks to Tina Soliman Hunter for starting this whole project and never quitting, even when it took a personal toll. And then there is my wife, Lori Nelsen, who has been there since the idea of studying the North Sea was just a seed. Trips to Britain and Norway followed, sometimes under less-than-ideal living conditions for a family. And now she has been my support through the writing of this book. The debt I owe her can never be repaid.

For me (Tina) the 'Brent Book' was the single most important tool I possessed when undertaking my PhD on offshore petroleum and the role of the state, and I am greatly indebted to Brent for not only writing the fabulous first iteration of this book, but also for agreeing to write an updated version. I deeply appreciate his time, patience, and guidance through this vast area, so that we might produce a book that is of the same vein as the first. Thanks must also go to the patient and brilliant editor at Edward Elgar, Ben Booth.

Of course, all of my analysis would be nothing without the insight and guidance of the titan of Norwegian petroleum law, Professor Ernst Nordtveit,

The North Sea system for petroleum production

who, over the last 20 years, has shaped my knowledge, and enabled me to apply logic and reason to this area of law, and in some small way contribute. I also must thank those on the other side of the pond, especially Professor John Paterson and Professor Greg Gordon.

Finally, I recognise the sacrifice of all those who have given their lives in the quest for North Sea oil and gas. May the souls of those men from the Piper Alpha, the *Alexander Kielland*, numerous dive bells, and platforms that have lost their lives, rest in peace. May our quest for oil and gas production incorporate state intervention that makes this activity as safe as possible for all who follow.

Abbreviations

APA	Pre-Defined Area (Norway)
APRT	Advanced Petroleum Revenue Tax (UK)
BEIS	Department for Business, Energy and Industrial Strategy (UK)
BGC	British Gas Corporation
BNOC	British National Oil Corporation
BP	British Petroleum
CCS	Carbon capture and storage
CCUS	Carbon capture, usage, and storage
CoP	Conference of Parties
DECC	Department of Energy and Climate Change (UK)
DoE	Department of Energy (UK)
DTI	Department of Trade and Industry (UK)
EC	European Community
EEA	European Economic Area
EFTA	European Free Trade Association
EOR	Enhanced oil recovery
EPL	Energy Profits Levy (UK)
EU	European Union
GB Energy	Great British Energy
GFU	Gas Negotiation Committee (Norway)
HSE	Health, safety, and environmental
IEA	International Energy Agency
IOC	International oil company
IOR	Improved oil recovery
JOA	Joint Operating Agreement
LNG	Liquified natural gas

LO	Norwegian Confederation of Trade Unions
MER UK	Maximize Economic Recovery (UK)
MoP	Ministry of Power (UK)
MOU	Memorandum of understanding
MPE	Ministry of Petroleum and Energy (Norway)
NAM	Dutch Petroleum Company
NATO	North Atlantic Treaty Organization
NCS	Norwegian Continental Shelf
NHO	Norwegian Business Association
NIFO	Norwegian Industry Association for Oil Companies
NOA	National Oil Account (UK)
NPD	Norwegian Petroleum Directorate
NSTA	North Sea Transition Authority (UK)
OEUK	Offshore Energies Association UK
OFGAS	Office of Gas Supply
OGA	Oil and Gas Authority (UK)
OPA	Oil and Pipelines Agency (UK)
OPEC	Organization of Petroleum Exporting Countries
OSO	Offshore Supplies Office (UK)
PAA	Petroleum Activities Act 1996 (Norway)
PAC	Public Accounts Committee (UK)
PAR	Petroleum Activities Regulations 1997 (Norway)
PDO	Plan for development and operation
PRT	Petroleum Revenue Tax (UK)
PSPLA	*Petroleum and Submarine Pipe-Line Act* (UK)
RFCT	Ring-Fence Corporation Tax (UK)
SC	Supplementary Charge (UK)
SDFI	State's Direct Financial Interest (Norway)
SPD	Supplementary Petroleum Duty (UK)
SV	Socialist Left Party (Norway)
TPA	Third-Party Access
UK	United Kingdom
UKCS	United Kingdom Continental Shelf

UKOOA	United Kingdom Offshore Operators Association
UN	United Nations
UNCLOS	*United Nations Convention on the Law of the Sea, 1982*
UNFCCC	UN Framework Convention on Climate Change
US	United States of America

1.   Framework: explaining state intervention offshore

Susan Strange (1988, p. 11), the great political economist of a previous generation, once wrote: a 'theory [of international politics] must seek to explain some aspect of the international system that is not easily explained by common sense. It must explain a puzzle or a paradox where there is some aspect of the behaviour of individuals, groups or social institutions for which a simple explanation is not apparent'. North Sea petroleum policy presents an interesting puzzle that Professor Strange might have appreciated. Two West European states with long intertwined histories – the UK and Norway – both found oil beneath the seabed at the same time under the same waters they had plied for centuries as fishers, traders, explorers, and marauders. Initially both states established light regulatory regimes in the 1960s designed to encourage private exploration for petroleum deposits. In the 1970s, this light touch evolved into stricter regimes that included special taxes, state participation in offshore production activities, and public ownership of petroleum companies. Then, as the 1970s faded into the 1980s, policy diverged. The British state pulled back from the offshore petroleum business and contented itself with regulating private offshore activity. The Norwegian state, meanwhile, continued and even increased, active participation in the offshore sector. So, that is a puzzle. What changed? And why over time have the two policy regimes reconverged in important ways? That is what this book is about.

Before we get to the 'why' question, we will have to describe the 'what'. In our (admittedly biased) opinion, the story of North Sea petroleum policy is rather gripping. It's a tale of swashbuckling Texas oil men colliding with stone-faced bureaucrats; it's the disappointment of umpteen dry wells, followed by the elation of billion-dollar gushers; it's the fear of big storms and 100-year waves; it's the saving of dying communities, the promise of hard work at good pay, the satisfaction of building huge new structures; and it's the tragedy of lives lost offshore. And for those of us who take great interest in the human struggle to govern our immensely complex societies, this is the story of how men and women, often pursuing very different interests, came to manage – imperfectly for sure – the risks and rewards of offshore petroleum development. Thus, this book addresses the puzzle of offshore policy by telling an interesting story.

But we also address the puzzle by answering the 'why' question. We are not breaking new theoretical ground in this study. Rather, we employ a small set of standard theoretical tools to help us understand why policy evolved the way it did in Britain and Norway. We believe these tools apply to offshore petroleum policy – we leave it to others to determine their general utility. Our aim is to provide students, state practitioners, commercial players, and historians with a practical guide to the evolution of offshore petroleum policy in Britain and Norway, with an eye to the forces that pressed policy makers in both countries to create offshore regimes that ultimately diverged in important ways.

COMPARING POLICIES

Before describing our explanatory framework, we need to define some important terms. We begin with the primary topic of this book, offshore petroleum policy.

Offshore petroleum policy is the set of rules established by relevant state authorities that apply to the exploitation of hydrocarbon deposits beneath the seabed in territory recognized internationally as the exclusive economic domain of a particular sovereign nation-state. These rules cover the four phases of oil and gas production: exploration, development, production, and abandonment. *Exploration* involves the search for commercially exploitable oil and gas deposits. The process involves extensive surveying of the ocean floor and the rock formations below. Teams of geologists using the computing power, data storage, and artificial intelligence expertise of the tech giants (Eder, 2019) select the sites for exploratory drilling they judge most promising – and then analyze the results. Drilling crews head offshore to sink these exploratory wells using a variety of methods involving stationary drilling ships, semi-submersible vessels (drilling platforms mounted on two submarines that can submerge below the surface churn), and an increasing amount of automation and subsea robotics. Governments usually have an interest in encouraging exploration, but not to the detriment of good order. Keeping order offshore requires governments to license operators and enforce rules regulating exploration activities, worker safety, environmental protection, and data sharing.

The *development* phase begins once the licensee (usually a consortium of companies led by a designated 'operator') declares the field commercially viable and announces its intention to produce the newly discovered hydrocarbons. The operator then takes responsibility for planning, financing, and building the material and human infrastructure necessary to bring the field into service. Such a task is daunting and costly[1] even for the largest, most experienced petroleum companies. Extreme conditions, especially in the far north, present challenges for engineers searching for cost-effective approaches to deep-sea production that also protect workers and the environment. Consortia in the early decades of offshore production built massive cities in the sea and mounted them on steel or concrete bases, some of which stood taller than the Eiffel Tower and the Empire State Building.[2] Advances in automated subsea production now make it possible to limit the number of individuals living offshore. Snøhvit, for instance, the northernmost petroleum production site on the Norwegian Continental Shelf (NCS), has no offshore surface installations whatsoever (Jacobsen, 2010, p. 267). The personnel needed to run the site are all located on shore at the landing installation on Melkøya, an island connected by tunnel to Hammerfest. Similarly, production from the giant Ormen Lange gas field located in the Norwegian Sea in 1000 meters of water – and which supplies more that 25 percent of Britain's gas needs – has been developed using 24 subsea wells in four seabed templates. The wells are then connected directly to the onshore processing facility at Nyhanma by two, 30-inch transportation pipelines which traverse the steeply inclined Storegga Slide (Shell, 2023). While responsibility for developing a field rests primarily with the offshore licensee, once again, government officials have an interest in regulating every aspect of the development phase, including the planning of infrastructure, the use of local products and labor, the landing of the petroleum, and the start date for production – as well as the human and environmental protections built into the plans.

The *production* phase begins when the hydrocarbons start to flow, although there is usually overlap with the development phase as most fields are built out in stages over several years, or decades. Hydrocarbon production gradually increases as more networked production wells are drilled and transport pipelines are connected to the central hub. Production generally rises steeply to a peak production level within ten years of a field's first deliveries, followed by a more gradual decline. New geologic information and advances in petroleum recovery technology may extend the life of a field long past its originally predicted expiration. Ekofisk on the NCS, for instance, began producing in 1971 and reached an initial peak in 1976. But continued development (the complex now includes 29 platforms) and improved recovery techniques led to a second spike in production to a new peak in the early 2000s. The field

---

[1]   Johan Sverdrup, one of Norway's newest fields, cost $9.2 billion to bring online in October 2019 (Fraser, 2019).
[2]   The Troll A platform, which was placed on the Norwegian Continental Shelf in 1996, still holds the record for the tallest and heaviest structure ever moved across the face of the earth ('Troll A platform', *Wikipedia*).

now may continue producing through 2050. Governments in this phase are primarily interested in securing their fair share of the revenue through taxation and return on any investments they may have made in the offshore sector. They also continue to enforce safety and environmental regulations.

The final phase in the production of petroleum is *abandonment*. At some point, it becomes unprofitable to continue producing hydrocarbons from a particular well or field. At this point, the licensees decide to decommission the installation. Abandonment is costly if the offshore structures must be removed entirely from the seabed – a prospect licensees would prefer to avoid. Governments, however, have an interest in getting this phase right. They must set rules for decommissioning equipment that protect workers and the environment. They also must make sure fields are not prematurely abandoned and companies have enough resources to pay for the clean-up. This is a tough job when consortia have no direct financial incentive to spend money on decommissioning. Getting them to do so requires government vigilance. During this final phase in production states typically increase both the level of state intervention, and the type of intervention (see Chapter 4).

As is apparent from the discussion above, states have an interest in each phase of petroleum production. At a minimum, the state is anxious to maintain order on its continental shelf, but beyond that, it also seeks to maximize revenues from the exploitation of its natural resources. In addition, the state maintains an interest in boosting job creation and economic development, expanding technical expertise, and ensuring human and environmental safety. States, however, can and have adopted different strategies – over time and between countries – to achieve these goals. The key variable is the extent to which the state intervenes in offshore petroleum activities. States have the right to intervene offshore because they hold sovereign rights over the resources. But should they try to produce and sell the oil and gas themselves, or should they outsource part or all the petroleum production process to experienced international oil companies (IOCs)? If they outsource, how much control should they maintain over private company activities? If they participate in the offshore industry, how much of the industry should they own? Should state shares be used to implement government policy, or should the state interest behave like a private commercial enterprise? States must balance their interests and navigate sometimes conflicting roles when determining their level of intervention offshore (Hunter, 2011).

Three types of involvement have emerged over time in the North Sea: minimal, regulatory, and participatory intervention. States adopting *minimal* intervention assume the role of offshore referee. Officials distribute territory to private enterprises that agree to abide by rules governing their activities. The rules bring order to the phases of production by regulating offshore competition, setting basic operating rules that protect workers and the environment, and reaping some of the offshore profits. Companies control most of the exploration process, field development plans, production levels, and platform abandonment. The state has a say in all important issues, but it guides with a light touch to encourage private companies to invest heavily in offshore exploration and development.

A state that adopts *regulatory* intervention assumes the role of offshore overseer. State officials do not watch offshore activity from the sidelines; they are present and actively shaping every aspect of oil and gas production. The state writes and monitors rules governing each phase of production, scrutinizes and approves every major action taken by the petroleum companies, influences the rate of hydrocarbon production, and implements a special tax regime that benefits the state treasury and intentionally creates incentives to guide company behavior. Comprehensive regulatory intervention ensures that state interests play an important, even decisive role in the decisions of private companies.

Finally, states adopting *participatory* intervention assume the role of offshore business participant. In this case,

> the state develops or maintains all its duties as overseer but goes a step further by entering the petroleum business as an entrepreneur. The state enters the industry as a shareholder and active participant for the purpose of acquiring greater control of offshore activities, gaining expertise and inside information, and not least, adding to its offshore tax revenues by turning a profit. (Nelsen, 1991, p. 9; see also Klapp, 1987)

State petroleum enterprises act as an additional tool for government officials to use in pursuit of their policy goals. The state is thus able to control offshore activities from both inside and outside the industry.

The types of intervention that emerged in the North Sea represented a progressive deepening of state involvement in offshore activities. But the types do not represent sequential steps; states do not have to begin with minimal intervention, move to regulatory intervention, and finally land on participatory intervention. While there is certainly a degree of path dependence, states can and do skip through the types. As we will see in the chapters that follow, Britain and Norway first adopted minimal intervention on the continental shelf but moved to participatory intervention in the 1970s. Norway modified its brand of participatory intervention, but stuck with the overall policy type, while Britain spent the 1980s dismantling the state's participatory role offshore and shoring up its regulatory regime. By the end of the 1980s, the two states had settled into policies of different types – Norway with a participatory and Britain with a regulatory system. Later, Norway backed away from much – but not all – of its participation on the NCS, and Britain moved to a more directed regulatory regime closer to that found in Norway.

EXPLAINING POLICY VARIATION

The purpose of this study is to explain the variation in offshore state intervention (type of intervention) over time and between two countries, Britain
and Norway. Our explanatory framework (see Figure 1.1) is quite simple:
the choice of policy type is the product of discussions between key players
in offshore activities whose bargaining positions are shaped by three external
(exogenous) factors – conditions present in the global hydrocarbon system,
organized economic and political interests (domestic and international), and
national political cultures. Policy is never made in a vacuum; we here make
explicit the pressures filling the void.

Figure 1.1   Explanatory framework

Real men and women, who are employed by public and private institutions
with interests in policy outcomes, interact to make offshore oil and gas policy.
As Øystein Noreng pointed out in 1980, these individuals operate at three
different levels – the petroleum, domestic political, and international levels
(Noreng, 1980, pp. 110–111; Nelsen, 1992, p. 312). Policy makers focus on
different issues and adopt distinctive goals when interacting at each level.
First, at the *petroleum level*, state policy officials make decisions based on the
requirements of the petroleum market and what the industry deems 'good oil
field practice'. The primary objective is to find and produce petroleum. The
companies will aim for efficiency and profitability, while the state will look for
ways to reap increased revenues and political credit. At this level, the state's
ability to benefit from offshore activity will be determined by the interest of
the petroleum companies in operating in the area; the more desperate they
are, the more willing they will be to agree to conditions they might otherwise
deem onerous. Second, at the *domestic political level*, governments are subjected to conflicting pressures from a variety of interested organizations and
political parties. Policy makers at this level are 'essentially concerned with
the government's ability to survive and maintain freedom of action' even as it

is pulled in different directions (Noreng, 1980, p. 110). Governments, which in parliamentary democracies are held accountable by their electorates for economic performance, must please key political constituencies, economic interests, coalition partners, and competing political parties. Thus, at this level, organized interests, self-interested politicians, and career bureaucrats struggle for control of government policy. Politicians will have to satisfy the interests most politically important, while officials will pursue the interests of the state bureaucracies they serve.

Finally, at an *international level,* policy makers consider the global political context when shaping policy. Petroleum fuels economic development and growth in every country on the planet. Petroleum-poor countries require transnational shipments and low prices to thrive economically; petroleum-rich countries require high global demand and high prices to prosper. Thus, oil and gas become foreign policy issues for many countries. The price of oil, the number of suppliers in the market, and international conflicts can alter the ability of nation-states to satisfy their citizens. The international context can alter the relationship between the petroleum companies and governments, and consuming countries can put pressure on producing states to lower prices or enforce sanctions (e.g., embargoes). Policy makers must consider the global situation and their country's foreign policy goals when determining how much to intervene offshore.

Policy makers are not operating on every level all the time. When petroleum companies first take an interest in a potential oil province, decisions are made almost exclusively at the petroleum level. Some domestic concerns may seep into the discussions between company representatives and state officials, but for the most part, the issues are confined to ensuring orderly exploration and 'good oil field practice'. As an oil province matures, economic and political interests awaken and policy makers, including political leaders, come under pressure to satisfy important constituencies. At this point, policy makers are operating on both the petroleum and domestic political levels. Finally, if a province becomes so productive that it starts influencing the global oil and gas markets, other producing and consuming countries take an interest and policy makers begin operating on all three levels. The three-level process may continue for several years, but it is very likely the three distinct levels will rise and fall in importance over time. For instance, when petroleum markets are stable and geopolitical conflicts at a minimum, the international level may diminish in importance leaving policy makers to consider only the technical requirements of the offshore sector (petroleum level) and domestic political ramifications of policy decisions (domestic political level). Or, for another example, a declining petroleum province may lose its international impact and much of its domestic political influence. At this point, policy makers are only concerned that companies maintain 'good oil field practice' while decommissioning fields.

Each policy level presents decision makers with a different set of bargaining partners. At the petroleum level, state officials deal almost exclusively with representatives of major oil and gas companies. At the domestic political level, state officials must sit across the table from interest group envoys, political party representatives, as well as petroleum company officials. To complicate matters further, different state agencies may have distinct interests, which must be satisfied through the decision-making process. And, of course, all of these groups – state and non-state alike – also engage in discussions among themselves. Finally, at the international level, state officials must respond to foreign governments and multilateral organizations (both those the country has joined, and those it has not).

Thus, state decision makers, on each level, find themselves locked in discussions with their counterparts. Their ability to achieve state goals in these fora depends on the relative strength of their bargaining positions. The strength of their positions depends, in turn, on factors pressing the state policy-making institutions. We divide these factors into three categories: system conditions, organized pressure, and political culture. The central question we ask is, 'What factors favor greater state intervention on the continental shelf?'

We first consider *system conditions*. System conditions refer to the environment within which interactions between state officials and other actors take place. The following environmental characteristics are most important to the state's bargaining strength:

1. *Information Distribution*: State officials are disadvantaged when petroleum companies have access to more technical information about the continental shelf and petroleum production technology and processes than they do. Correcting that informational imbalance – or better yet, overcorrecting in the state's favor – puts state officials in a strong position to bargain with their company counterparts.
2. *Legal Framework*: State officials are in a stronger position if a legal framework for managing private-sector activity (including the allocation of territory, the assessment of taxes and fees, the enforcement of safety procedures, etc.) is already in place, no matter how rudimentary. In rule-of-law systems, appeals to existing legal principles and precedents strengthens the hand of state officials.
3. *Bureaucratic Capacity*: States will successfully intervene on the continental shelf only if they have created appropriate government agencies, adequately staffed them with talented, technically trained, bribe-resistant civil servants, and fully funded their operations.

4. *Petroleum Independence*: The less dependent a country is on petroleum for its energy needs, the more freedom state officials have to pressure companies for concessions that might slow production.

5. *Oil Price*: High petroleum prices raise company demand for offshore territory by increasing profit margins and making marginal finds commercially viable. State officials obtain leverage over companies when prices are high, and companies are eager to drill.

6. *Maturity of the Province*: Before a petroleum province is proven to contain commercially viable deposits, state officials have little leverage over the companies. Once a province is known to contain large amounts of oil and a gas boom occurs, then the bargaining power of state officials increases. A province on the wane gradually shifts leverage back to the companies.

7. *Province Competition*: State officials have more leverage when they control an entire province. In provinces divided by two or more national jurisdictions, state officials find themselves in regulatory competition with neighboring provinces. Since many petroleum companies are active globally, every province is exposed to some competition from other jurisdictions. Companies will generally prefer areas with less state intervention.

8. *Producer Cartels*: Effective international petroleum producer cartels will disadvantage private companies. International *consumer* cartels have not proven effective, but in theory they would also increase the leverage of state officials.

To put all of this together, state officials are freest (in relation to the petroleum companies) to intervene offshore in pursuit of government policy goals when they have access to information, oversee an existing legal framework, possess adequate bureaucratic capacity, enjoy some independence from oil to meet energy demands, experience high oil prices, govern a booming petroleum province with little competition from other provinces, and operate in a global market influenced by an international producer cartel (even if not a member). These conditions did not exist in the early years of North Sea petroleum exploration, which disadvantaged the British and Norwegian states. But the system changed dramatically in the 1970s after Middle Eastern oil states took control of their petroleum industries and successfully raised global prices and major oil and gas finds in the North Sea sparked a bonanza. British and Norwegian officials were suddenly in a position to win concessions from the oil companies. Systemic conditions changed again in the late twentieth century requiring new shifts in policy as state officials gave up some of their leverage.

Organized pressure – if it is not associated with the petroleum companies or offshore suppliers – almost always pushes state officials to intervene more deeply in offshore activities. *Interest groups* representing offshore workers, fishers, the environment, coastal communities, and other interests press the state to tilt policy in their direction. *State bureaucracies,* which pursue interests of their own, usually press for more control over high-impact industries. *Political parties*, of course, differ on the benefits of state intervention. But no party wants to be held responsible for a lapse in health or environmental safety, a failure to secure a fair share of offshore revenues, or an unwillingness to steer offshore business to domestic suppliers. Thus, political parties on both the left and the right tend to favor government management of the continental shelf, even as they differ on the means of achieving state goals. *Public opinion* – when aroused – usually presses the government to take a more active role in furthering domestic interests over foreign companies. Finally, external pressure from *foreign governments* and *multinational organizations* also encourages governments to intervene offshore, but usually in opposition to most domestic interests. Policy makers, thus, find themselves pressured by groups to intervene, often from diametrically opposing perspectives. These interests are themselves influenced by systemic conditions – the oil price, the level of government information, petroleum independence, etc. – which affect their bargaining strength vis-à-vis the state. Clearly, the process is inherently complex.

One last factor must be brought into the discussion, which is sometimes decisive: national *political culture*. Policy makers bring to the process preferences and biases shaped by the political culture in which they were socialized. Not all national political cultures in the West are alike. They differ, for instance, on the preferred method for regulating industry: continental Europeans tend to issue detailed rules for companies to follow; Britain, on the other hand, prefers to set out goals and let companies decide how to meet them. In regulatory terms, this is the difference between the civil law 'principle-based' approach and the more didactic 'prescriptive' approach utilized by many common law countries such as the UK and Australia (Hunter, 2011). In any case, both state officials and politicians are influenced by their national political cultures, which can bias the process toward or against offshore state intervention.

CONCLUSION

Offshore petroleum policy in the North Sea presents us with an interesting puzzle: why do two countries, so much alike, operating in the same area, overseeing the same industry during the same period, find their policies diverging on the crucial issue of state involvement offshore? Our explanatory framework identifies the decision-making levels where the state and other interests interact, and the explanatory factors that influence those relationships. Government decisions emerge from this complex interaction. We seek to untangle the influences on petroleum policy decisions in the following chapters as we retell the story of North Sea oil from the exciting early days of exploration to the calmer days of gradual production decline to the new flurry of activity as policy makers try to maximize petroleum production while transitioning to clean energy.

2. Convergence: developing the North Sea system

The United Kingdom (UK) and Norway share a sea between them, organize their politics around Parliaments, democratic elections, and strong political parties, and allocate resources through a regulated private market and a progressive tax system. But none of this guaranteed that the two countries would develop similar offshore petroleum systems in the 1960s and 1970s. Britain was a postwar world power with a long relationship with the oil majors and a history of colonial rule in the oil-rich Middle East. It was also highly dependent on imported oil despite the presence of a small onshore oil province. Norway, on the other hand, was a newly independent (1905), small country with a history of neutrality and no global great-power intentions. It was also energy independent due to the abundance of hydroelectric capacity. Virtually no one believed Norway had exploitable petroleum deposits.[1] The fact that British and Norwegian offshore policy did converge around a general North Sea system does need explaining – as do the important variations each country brought to the system.

This chapter details the origins of the petroleum boom in the North Sea. It also describes the systems of governance designed to maximize the benefits of this bonanza without hampering the ability or willingness of experienced oil companies to develop the resources beneath the sea floor. During these early years, the policy choices of the two countries converged around a common system of governance. That convergence is what we seek to explain.

BEFORE THE NORTH SEA

Petroleum exploitation, from its earliest days, has been a commercial venture undertaken by oil companies driven to produce petroleum as profitably as possible. But the commercial exploitation of oil differed from country to country. In the United States (US), it was private corporations that engaged in domestic petroleum activities. As these companies grew beyond US borders to become

---

[1] In a letter to the Norwegian Ministry of Foreign Affairs in 1958, the Norwegian Geological Society declared, 'the chances of finding coal, oil, or sulfur on the continental shelf off the Norwegian coast can be discounted' (Offshore Norge, 2017).

Table 2.1   Comparative features of North American system and North Sea system

Feature	North American	North Sea
License and concession system used	√	√
Licenses granted using cash bidding or work program bidding for allocation of licenses	√	
Licenses granted using criteria set by state		√
Production sharing contracts used	√	
State sets legal framework for activities and lets companies determine production rates and methods (Minimal intervention)	√	
State sets legal framework for activities and stipulates how activities should be done (Regulatory intervention)		√
State exerts regulatory intervention AND participates in petroleum activities (Participatory intervention)		√
State exerts high level of control over aspects of petroleum exploitation		√

Source: Compiled by authors.

international oil companies (IOCs), they exploited petroleum in accordance with the terms of concessions offered by host countries. The UK took a different approach. The British state put national interests at the heart of petroleum development in the early twentieth century and established state-owned companies to produce oil in third party countries (particularly Persia) to supply its navy with bunker fuel. Thus, whereas US petroleum exploitation was driven by profit, UK exploitation was undertaken primarily to further geostrategic interests (Nelsen, 1991, p. 8).

The American approach to petroleum production coalesced into a 'North American system' (see Table 2.1). In most oil-producing countries, petroleum is owned by, or reserved for, the state, or in monarchies, 'the Crown'. In the US, by contrast, petroleum rights and ownership are not reserved to the state; the private landowners can own the rights to the mineral resources (including oil) that lie beneath their land – or these mineral interests can be severed from the land (Daintith, 2011). This private ownership of minerals also entitles the owners to take from the land anything under (or flowing into) their land under the 'rule of capture' (Daintith, 2011). This ownership of oil interests has, to a large extent, exerted influence on the role of the state in the exploration for and development of onshore, and later offshore, petroleum resources.

As petroleum resource exploitation shifted offshore, initially into the Gulf of Mexico, petroleum-producing states largely adopted their onshore approaches to state involvement. The US continued to adhere to the North American approach to resource development; American IOCs took the lead with little state interference. The role of the state and the method of allocating access to petroleum on the US Continental Shelf was firmly entrenched. Concepts such as the 'rule of capture' and 'private ownership of minerals' that dominate onshore petroleum development persisted offshore.

Characteristic of the North American system was a state strategy of minimal intervention. Historically (and contemporarily) the US approach to onshore and offshore activity has been to allow petroleum companies to operate with only a light regulatory touch from the state (Anderson and Kulander, 2015). The American state confines its role to that stipulated in the primary offshore legislative instrument, the *Outer Continental Shelf Lands Act 1958* (US), which establishes an auction system for granting petroleum leases, authorizes the collection of royalties, and sets rules for petroleum operations (exploration, production, and abandonment), including standards governing health, safety, and environmental protection. The state exerts no influence over petroleum production rates apart from the effects of meeting regulatory standards. Similar systems exist elsewhere, including Australia and Canada. In these jurisdictions, licenses are awarded to financially and technically qualified companies either through work program bidding or monetary auction.[2] Once production licenses have been awarded, the oil companies are left to control field depletion, relying on market forces and company economic imperatives to dictate the rate of extraction and the timing of field abandonment.[3] There is no state participation, either directly or in the form of a national oil company. Thus, like the US, Australia and Canada epitomize the North American system.

IN THE BEGINNING

Prior to the late 1950s, the North Sea was known only for its abundant fish and deadly winter storms. Its surface had been plied for millennia by traders and raiders – and fishermen, who harvested the sea life beneath its waves. But no one suspected that the sea still hid its greatest treasure. Fabulous wealth remained locked below waves, water, sand, and rock awaiting discovery. Finding and securing it would require the combined efforts of some of the

---

[2] For the award of licenses in Australia, refer to §§ 104-109 of the *Offshore Petroleum and Greenhouse Gas Exploration Act 2006* (Cth).

[3] The capacity of the Commonwealth to regulate the depletion of a field is regulated under Part 2.4 of the *Offshore Petroleum and Greenhouse Gas Exploration Act 2006* (Cth).

largest private enterprises and most sophisticated public organizations in the world. But at mid-century, none of this was yet known – or even yet dreamed (for early histories of North Sea exploration, see Callow, 1973; Birnie, 1975; MacKay and Mackay, 1975; Chapman, 1976; Hamilton, 1978; Keto, 1978; Williams, 1981; Corti and Frazer, 1983; Helle, 1984).

In the immediate postwar period, the problem with the North Sea – particularly the continental shelf beneath it – was that it was ungoverned. What order existed came by way of a set of loose international norms (customary international laws) that prohibited certain high crimes but left vague many of the rules controlling economic activity. The seabed beyond three or 12 or 200 nautical miles (states unilaterally delineated their portion of the continental shelf) simply was not governed by nation states or multilateral organizations. Legal uncertainty ruled the seas making long-term investment in economic activity too risky. In any case, few states had any knowledge of what existed on or below the seabed just off their coasts and few had the technology to begin exploring for riches.

All that changed at the close of the 1950s. In July 1959, NAM (Dutch Petroleum Company), a Dutch joint venture owned equally by Shell and Esso, discovered in the northeastern region of the Netherlands a field they named Groningen, the largest gas field in Europe. The discovery of this super giant and the geological knowledge gained through the project suddenly focused the attention of petroleum companies on the North Sea, an area previously rejected as a potential oil and gas province. One obvious obstacle was water depth, but recent advances in offshore exploration and production technologies had encouraged oil companies to consider deep-sea sites. While marine drilling had begun in the 1890s and was used successfully in the shallow waters of Lake Maracaibo in Venezuela, deep water drilling in potentially harsh weather conditions had only begun in earnest in the 1950s when the US opened the Gulf of Mexico to petroleum production. Due to these recent developments, it was now possible for oil companies to follow up the Groningen discovery with a strong push out to sea where legal anarchy still reigned.

Three oil 'majors' – Standard Oil of New Jersey (Esso), Royal Dutch/Shell, and British Petroleum (BP) – launched an exploration effort called 'Operation Seashell' that conducted seismic surveys in the southern North Sea in 1962. Soon nearly two dozen companies were surveying the seabed well beyond the reach of any regulatory authority. But surveys were one thing, drilling another. Companies needed a much clearer legal structure before they would risk massive amounts of money searching for oil they might not have the right to produce.

Key questions needed answers before exploration wells could be drilled. First, who governed what areas of the North Sea and the continental shelf beneath it? Second, who owned the resources on or below the seabed? Third, who was authorized to search for exploitable resources? And finally, what rules would regulate the exploration and production of oil and gas? In 1962, the oil companies asked somewhat surprised British and Norwegian government officials these questions. The answers they received created the ownership and regulatory regime we now know as the 'North Sea system' (Soliman Hunter, 2023).

Establishing a Legal Framework

For each government, the first item of business was to declare sovereignty over the economic resources on their respective continental shelves. In this instance, developments in international law offered a course of action. The first Conference on the Law of the Sea, held in Geneva in 1958, adopted an important United Nations (UN) agreement called the *Geneva Convention on the Continental Shelf 1958* (Geneva Convention), which allowed coastal states to declare sovereign rights over the resources on their continental shelves to a depth of 200 meters, or beyond if technology permitted.[4] Thus, in May 1963, Norway became the first nation to act on the Geneva Convention when it declared sovereignty in respect to natural resources on its adjacent subsea shelf,[5] 'to such extent as the depth of the sea permits the utilization of natural resources' (Keto, 1978, p. 70). The declaration conveniently ignored the 700-meter-deep Norwegian trench hugging Norway's southern coast, which geologists thought was caused by fluvial erosion from past glacial activity rather than plate tectonics, thus making it a feature of the continental shelf rather than a natural boundary. The British declared sovereignty over its own continental shelf one year later in May 1964,[6] by being the last nation needed to ratify the Geneva Convention. In March 1965, the UK and Norway agreed to establish the mid-lines between their shores (ignoring the trench) as the

---

[4]   The *United Nations Convention on the Law of the Sea, 1982* (UNCLOS) currently governs coastal and international waters. With the coming into force of UNCLOS in 1994, Art. 56 of UNCLOS granted sovereign rights to develop the seabed and sub-seabed natural resources in the Exclusive Economic Zone (beyond 12 nautical miles), although since the US has not ratified UNCLOS, it continues to assert sovereignty (and not sovereign rights) over the US Continental Shelf.
[5]   By the *Royal Decree of 31 May 1963 Relating to the Sovereignty of Norway over the Sea-Bed and Subsoil outside the Norwegian Coast.* It was followed by the *Royal Decree of 9 April 1965 relating to Exploration for and Exploitation of Petroleum Deposits in the Sea-Bed and its Subsoil on the Norwegian Continental Shelf.*
[6]   Under the *Petroleum Act 1934* (UK).

international boundary,[7] as outlined in the Convention (agreements between other littoral countries took somewhat longer) – much to Norway's relief.

The Geneva Convention helped settle the question of jurisdiction on the continental shelf. Addressing the remaining questions required legislation. Parliaments in both countries set about drafting and passing enabling legislation designed to set the major parameters governing offshore petroleum activities. Both the Storting's (Norwegian Parliament) *Act No. 12 of 21 June 1963 Relating to Exploration for and Exploitation of Submarine Natural Resources* and the British Parliament's *Continental Shelf Act, (April) 1964* make clear three principles:

1. the Crown (i.e., the state) owns the subsea resources,
2. the state may grant persons or entities the right to explore for and develop these resources,
3. the state has the right to issue regulations governing offshore activities.

In short order, nation states extended their exclusive governance to offshore territory and claimed ownership of its bounty. For petroleum companies the states had eliminated the anxiety and uncertainty of international anarchy.

Establishing a Regulatory System

Britain
British and Norwegian officials next set about establishing the rules for exploration on the continental shelf. The British were first to establish a regulatory system for several reasons. First, Britain was not starting from scratch; it had a regulatory structure in place for its limited land-based petroleum activities based on the *Petroleum (Production) Act 1934*. Second, British officials had a close working relationship with representatives of the major oil companies bringing in needed knowledge, but also opening them to pressures for speedy development of the resources. Finally, Britain was broke. It needed domestic petroleum production to address a balance of payments crisis by decreasing its demand for energy imports – the sooner the better. Thus in 1963 the Ministry of Power (MoP) formed a committee to draw up legislation establishing a licensing policy. The new committee, the PAC, issued a report after soliciting advice from a broad variety of sources, but it drew most heavily on the advice and expertise of two committees representing the major oil companies (*PAC*

---

[7]   *Agreement Between the Government of the United Kingdom of Great Britain and Northern Ireland and the Government of the Kingdom of Norway Relating to the Delimitation of the Continental Shelf between the two Countries* (UN Treaty No. 8043).

Report, 1973, p. 23). After studying the issues, the policy committee established four fundamental principles to guide decisionmakers:

1. 'encourage rapid and thorough exploration and economical development' of petroleum resources,
2. maximize the financial benefit to the Exchequer without discouraging oil company involvement,
3. set terms that would not 'react unfavorably' on the UK oil industry abroad, and
4. ensure 'adequate British representation' on the continental shelf. (*PAC Report,* p. 25)

Based on these principles, the MoP established a licensing system set down in the *Petroleum (Production) (Continental Shelf and Territorial Sea) Regulations, 1964.*

The 1964 system of allocating petroleum licenses – which in the main is still used today – was designed for speed and control. Regulators divided the UK Continental Shelf (UKCS) into relatively small blocks (250 sq. km) to encourage more thorough exploration and the involvement of smaller (often British) companies with limited resources (see Table 2.2). After some debate, officials decided to issue licenses at the discretion of the MoP rather than through an American-style auction system (Cameron, 1983; Frewer, 2000; Bunter, 2002; Hunter, 2015). An auction system, while lucrative in the long run, does not, as one official put it, 'permit the same range of detailed control that discretionary licensing systems do' (*PAC Report*, p. 3). Ministry officials in a discretionary system could hold companies to a rigorous, speedy exploration schedule and in subtle and not-so-subtle ways favor British industry. In short, a discretionary system allowed the Ministry to balance the sometimes-competing goals of speed, benefit to the Treasury, and British industrial development.

Licenses came in two types: exploration and production. Exploration licenses granted the license holder (who had to be a British resident, or a company incorporated in the UK) the non-exclusive right to explore a territory for three years for an annual fee and rights to the data. The license did not allow for drilling. Exploration licenses allowed the licensee to search for and recover oil and gas in a specific area for a total of 46 years. Applicants had to submit a six-year work program for a particular block, which soon became part of an unofficial bidding process as companies tried to impress officials with their aggressive exploration plans. After six years, production licensees were required to relinquish 50 percent of each block awarded to them. This provision benefited the state because it pressured companies to explore thoroughly their blocks, allowed other companies to take a look at relinquished territory, and permitted officials to amend the terms of territory previously licensed. License

Table 2.2   The first licensing systems

	Britain	Norway
Terms		
Block size	250 sq. km	500 sq. km
Types of Licenses	• Exploration • Production	• Reconnaissance • Production
Length of Production License	6+40 yrs	6+40 yrs
Relinquishment Requirement	50% after 6 yrs	25% after 6 yrs 25% after 3 yrs
Fees	Progressive	Progressive
Work Program	Yes	Yes
Allocation Method	Discretionary (1971-Auction)	Discretionary
Taxes		
Royalties	12.5%	10%
Taxes	Corporate Rate	Corporate Rate

Source: Nelsen (1991, p. 20). Used by permission.

fees also encouraged thorough exploration. For the first six years, a licensee paid a one-time fee of £25 per square kilometer (approximately £6250 per block). After relinquishing territory, licensees paid progressive fees on any remaining territory (up to £290 per sq. km) as an incentive to shed unproductive areas. Finally, an additional requirement obligated license holders to land in the UK any petroleum they produced on the UKCS, thus boosting British industry, ensuring energy supplies, and benefiting the balance of payments.

British officials understandably established a conservative offshore tax regime as an encouragement to investment. Offshore investors paid standard corporate income tax (originally 53.75 percent), plus an industry standard 12.5 percent royalty on petroleum produced, payable in cash or kind (i.e., oil). All in all, the government was set to take 50–60 percent of company offshore profits.

Norway

The Norwegians, at the same time, felt more and less hurried than the British in 1963. Phillips Petroleum had asked the Norwegian government for exclusive rights to the entire Norwegian Continental Shelf (NCS) in October 1962, with several more companies following right behind. Norwegian officials demurred and stalled for time. But the companies maintained their pressure. Thus, a month after declaring sovereignty over the continental shelf, the Norwegian government granted exploration licenses to Phillips and two consortia comprised of several of the oil majors. These licenses allowed the companies to conduct geological surveys but not to drill into the seabed. By rejecting Phillips' request for exclusive rights to the shelf and allowing several global petroleum producers to operate in its sector, the Norwegians declared to the world their openness to private investment and corporate competition, while simultaneously underlining the state's control of access to the NCS. They responded to oil company pressure to license the extremely attractive areas in the southern sector, but once that was done, officials were determined to take their time developing a comprehensive offshore regulatory regime.

The Norwegian government finally established its offshore system in April 1965. Norway had a history of issuing concessions to foreign companies looking to exploit Norwegian resources. Soon after complete independence in 1905, the Norwegian government, motivated by resource nationalism, intervened in the development of hydropower primarily to secure opportunities for fledgling Norwegian companies. The Minister of Justice, Johan Castberg (Labour Democrats), made very clear his views on foreign companies exploiting Norway's hydroelectric resources:

> We have in our natural resources greater riches than any other country in Europe. The rain of heaven, which is naturally stored up on the mountains like white coals, is a wealth which we will not cast out like scraps to foreign vultures. We will not give away to foreign capital that which can be used for our common benefit. (Castberg, 1912)

The Concession laws regulated access to watercourses in Norway to prevent large foreign corporations from controlling Norwegian natural resources. Under the 1909 Concession Law, foreign corporations were granted a concession (i.e., the consent of the Norwegian government) to purchase rights to develop a watercourse for hydropower for a period (usually 60–80 years) whereupon the private interest (including any improvements to the land) would revert to the state without compensation paid to the concession holders (Sanders, 2023). The level of state intervention increased with the 1917 Watercourse Concession Law, which required, among other things, that concession holders pay the state licensing fees so all Norwegians could benefit from hydroelectric development (Sanders, 2023). The same fears that motivated Norway to intervene in hydropower development haunted Norwegian officials facing the prospects of a rush for offshore petroleum. Producing oil and gas seemed like a business foreign investors were even more likely to dominate. Norway was much smaller than the UK and was entirely dependent on international capital to develop resources found offshore. Nevertheless, British offshore policies heavily influenced the details of the Norwegian system (see Table 2.2). Where the systems differed, the Norwegian scheme attempted to lure investment with easier terms than those offered by Britain.

Like Britain, Norway adopted a discretionary licensing system to better control offshore activities (Taverne, 1999; Davis, 2004). Officials never seriously considered auctioning licenses. Two types of licenses were offered: reconnaissance (Britain's 'exploration') and production.[8] Reconnaissance licenses gave holders nonexclusive rights to explore (without drilling) designated areas for a fee. Production licenses, like their British counterparts, ran for a total of 46 years and required applicants to reside (or have their 'seat') in Norway, apply for specific blocks, and commit to a six-year work program approved by the Ministry of Industry. Officials understood that the NCS was less attractive to companies than the British sector, so it offered several incentives to attract interest. First, the blocks offered were double the size of the British blocks (500 sq. kms). Second, licensees were required after six years to relinquish only one-fourth of their territory, with an additional 25 percent to be surrendered after three more years. This allowed licensees nine years to explore their blocks before giving back 50 percent to the Norwegian state. Third, the Norwegian fee structure offered NCS license holders a slightly better deal per kilometer than on the UKCS. In addition, the discount on Norwegian blocks carried over into the tax structure where the Ministry set the royalty rate at 10 percent (in part to offset the longer distances to shore), paid in cash or kind at the Ministry's discretion, based on a negotiated base rate rather than each company's reported price information. Normal corporate taxes also applied, so the Norwegian state was taking between 54 and 57 percent of oil company profits, which was a bit more attractive than the British tax take.

Where the Norwegian sector was less attractive to oil companies than the British sector was in offshore safety. The British were content to set broad principles for protecting workers and the environment and let the companies develop their own systems to meet the goals. Not so the Norwegians. By 1967 they had set specific and stringent regulations governing every aspect of offshore activity and assigned a number of directorates and boards to enforce the rules. Safety was not an area where Norwegian officials took the competitiveness of the NCS into consideration.

Institutional Structures

Licensing regulations were very important to the early British and Norwegian offshore regimes, but so were the institutional structures established in the early 1960s. In Britain, the licensing policy was developed in 1963 by a small

---

[8]   Britain now issues a different set of licenses. See Chapter 4.

committee of administrators and legal experts within the MoP. In 1964, the committee – still very small – had become the Petroleum Division of the MoP. In 1969, the Ministry of Technology absorbed it, and a year later the Department of Trade and Industry (DTI) took it in. In Norway, a small committee of civil servants and scientists developed the licensing system. This advisory committee was formally established in 1965 as the Norwegian Petroleum Council (with members added representing industry and local government), which was to advise the Ministry of Industry. The Council became a key element of the Norwegian system – in fact the center of petroleum policymaking – involved in everything from licensing to safety regulations. Over time, it developed the information resources and expertise to challenge the oil companies when the state sought greater control.

First Licensing Rounds

The British government was the first to offer companies the opportunity to acquire North Sea licenses. In April 1964 – before the North Sea boundaries were yet agreed – the MoP announced its criteria for awarding licenses: the proposed work program (and ability to implement it), and the proposed contribution to the development of offshore petroleum resources and Britain's overall fuel economy (*PAC Report*, 1973, p. 26). Companies realized that these criteria were the 'currency' needed to bid for blocks on the UKCS. Thus, in May 1964, Britain held its first licensing round offering 960 blocks, virtually all its available territory. Companies applied for 394 blocks, with the Ministry awarding 53 licenses covering 348 blocks. Rigs were on the shelf just after Christmas 1964.

   Just before drilling started, however, the Labour party won the October 1964 General Election and formed a new government under Harold Wilson. Labour reviewed the policies of the previous Conservative government and decided not to change the offshore system in any substantial way. But the government did decide to hold a second licensing round that would include territory up against the newly agreed international borders. Following precedent, the government announced early its decision criteria for the round; it confirmed previous criteria but added three more: past performance, contribution to the economy, and participation of state enterprises. This last criterion introduced a new element to the offshore system; consortia of petroleum companies now knew they had to seek state-owned partners. The Gas Council was a state monopoly with control of the onshore town gas (gas derived from coal) distribution system and the right of first refusal (in fact, monopsony power) on any gas discovered on the UKCS. It was also a partner in several First Round licenses and joined Second Round partnerships with consortia eager to please the Ministry. The Council raised its stake in these new partnerships to 50 percent. The Second

Round, employing these new criteria, did not go particularly well: the government offered 1100 blocks, but companies applied for only 127. The mood, however, soon changed. In September 1965, just before companies learned the results of the Second Round, BP struck a sizable gas field it named West Sole. By 1967, exploration activities yielded three more major gas fields.

The North Sea petroleum bonanza was clearly underway, but natural gas presents companies with a problem, price. Before the development of technology that enabled the liquifying and transporting of gas in tankers, which created a global market in natural gas, producers were required to build gas pipelines, which limited the number of possible buyers. In Britain, the Gas Council was the sole buyer of gas, meaning the price had to be directly negotiated with the companies on a field-by-field basis; no open market in gas existed. Since the Gas Council participated in several production consortia *and* served as the monopsony buyer, it effectively sat on both sides of the bargaining table when establishing a price. Its challenge was to negotiate a price low enough to offer British households and industry real economic advantages without discouraging exploration in the UK offshore sector. The Council met fierce resistance from the companies but, in the end, it used a divide-and-conquer approach to force companies with smaller gas deposits to reach a settlement with the Council. Companies with bigger finds were forced to follow suit. By the end of the 1960s, the UK sector was producing significant amounts of natural gas and selling it at a price essentially set by the state.

The Norwegians took their time in granting IOCs greater access to the NCS for petroleum exploration, holding their first licensing round a year later than the British (April 1965). The round offered almost every block in the Norwegian sector (278) but attracted only 11 applications. After some hard negotiations over work programs, the Ministry of Industry awarded 22 licenses to nine groups covering 78 blocks. After making awards utilizing its discretion, the Ministry announced its assessment criteria: applicant's financial strength, practical experience, contribution to the Norwegian economy, Norwegian composition, and work program. None of these criteria surprised the companies, given the government's prior indications that Norwegian interests were high priorities.

Exploration on the NCS began in July 1966. The first well was dry, as were all the wells that year, and the next. Not surprisingly, oil company interest began to wane. In June 1968, however, Phillips Petroleum found a small gas condensate field that was subsequently named Cod. This small field piqued interest, but both the company and the Ministry deemed it uncommercial. The Ministry then held a second licensing round in September 1968 offering 68 blocks under the same criteria as the First Round. License conditions might be the same, but thinking in the Ministry was beginning to change. The Cod find proved that some hydrocarbons existed on the NCS. Moreover, some governments of the newly established Organization of Petroleum Exporting Countries (OPEC), led by Saudi Arabia and Iraq, had declared their intention to take a direct interest in oil production. Norwegian officials, intrigued by this shift to host-government intervention, began considering the possibility of introducing state involvement in offshore petroleum activities. In December 1968, the cabinet directed the Petroleum Council to negotiate state participation agreements with applicants to the second licensing round. The companies cried foul; the Norwegians were changing the rules in the middle of the game – to some oil men they were acting like 'Blue-eyed Arabs' (Helle, 1984, p. 71). Several applicants to the second licensing round withdrew, resulting in only six applicants receiving licenses. Despite its unpopularity among foreign oil executives, however, this swivel to the Middle East was to influence the future of state intervention on the NCS.

Meanwhile, companies working the NCS were drilling nothing but dry holes.

In late 1969, Phillips sank the 33rd well on the NCS. Early on, the well ran into problems and Phillips abandoned it, stating that it would not redrill this well. Norwegian authorities, however, insisted that Phillips carry out its work program and drill the final well. Grumbling about the futility of it all, the company reluctantly moved a few meters away and set to drilling a second well. On 23 December 1969 Phillips struck a giant oil and gas reservoir it named Ekofisk. Norway had the Christmas present of the century! – a giant oil field later assessed to contain over four billion barrels of oil, which today continues to produce more than 130 000 b/d.

Assessing the First Systems

We turn to our explanatory framework to help us explain the policy actions of the British and Norwegians in the early years of petroleum activities on the continental shelf. In the British sector, most of the system conditions put government officials in a relatively weak position vis-à-vis the petroleum companies (see Figure 2.1): the province was attractive but unproven; crude prices, while low, did not matter much in a province where no oil had yet been found; and Britain was desperate for domestic supplies of oil and gas. Mitigating factors, however, offered the state some resources to improve its bargaining position. Experience with domestic petroleum production and good relations with major oil companies – in particular the partially state-owned BP and the private Anglo-Dutch Shell, key players in the Persian Gulf – offered state officials access to important expertise and several legal and regulatory precedents to build upon. Organized pressure on decision makers did not influence policy very much. The one exception was political parties. Labour's decision to introduce state participation in the Second Round and its pressure on companies to accept a lower gas price foreshadowed greater party influence in the future. But for the most part, British policy making was unaffected by political interests apart from the interests directly engaged in offshore activities. As for national norms, British policy makers were primarily influenced by the need for speed, which favored a less regulated offshore sector. The British were historically predisposed to favor the market, but Fabian socialism with its emphasis on state ownership of key industries and Keynesian demand management remained significant intellectual forces in 1960s Britain. The early years, however, only saw hints of greater state involvement on the UKCS.

Figure 2.1   Early years: Britain

Early British petroleum policy making remained at the level where the primary relationship was between state officials and interested petroleum companies. The absence of system conditions favorable to state intervention and interest groups willing to counter company pressure ensured the British offshore regime met the characteristics of *minimal state intervention* in these early years.

The same was roughly true in Norway at the same time (see Figure 2.2). The Norwegian state had a concessions system in which to ground its offshore licensing policy, but it lacked independent information of the NCS. Due to the abundance of hydroelectric power in Norway, the country was little dependent on imported petroleum and thus not focused on speedy offshore development. But the Norwegian sector was less attractive to the IOCs than the UKCS, which disadvantaged the state in its negotiations. Neither organized interests nor political parties took much interest in Norwegian petroleum developments in the early years although the state bureaucracy – consistent with more interventionist national norms – looked for chances to exert greater influence over the system. State officials succeeded in creating a rigorous offshore safety system over the resistance of the companies, a development consistent with national norms. All in all, Norway's offshore system may have been a bit more orderly and government directed (note the insistence on drilling that last well over Ekofisk!) than Britain's. But the differences were minor; British and Norwegian offshore policies had *converged* to forge a common minimally interventionist system.

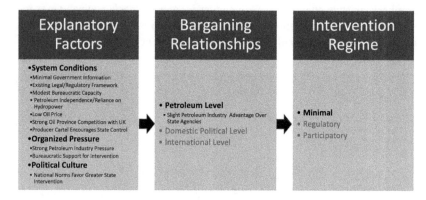

Figure 2.2   Early years: Norway

THE NORTH SEA SYSTEM TRANSFORMED

The 1970s was a tumultuous decade for the global petroleum industry: events fundamentally shifted power away from companies toward states. The discovery of Ekofisk transformed the North Sea from a marginally successful gas province with oil potential, to a proven (albeit high-cost) oil province with abundant gas as well. For the companies, the new North Sea play was almost too good to be true: large quantities of oil and gas were waiting to be discovered close to western markets under the sovereign control of stable, market-oriented democracies with trustworthy institutions. Greater industry demand for British and Norwegian offshore territory, however, weakened the bargaining power of companies (now competing for choice blocks) vis-à-vis state officials and politicians suddenly aware that a system designed to encourage private sector activity might not offer the state enough control to ensure tangible benefits to the domestic economy.

But worse was yet to come for petroleum companies. On 6 October 1973, war broke out between Israel and its Arab neighbors. On 13 October, negotiations broke down between OPEC and the major oil companies over the 'posted price' (the tax reference price) for crude oil. OPEC took full control of the pricing system and raised the per barrel price from approximately $3 to $5.11. On 17 October, OPEC agreed to cut oil shipments to Europe and ban exports entirely to the US and the Netherlands in retaliation for their resupplying of Israel during the war. The embargo put further pressure on prices, so on 22 December 1973, OPEC raised the barrel price to $11.65. Five years later the drama continued with the fall of the Shah of Iran in late 1978 and the outbreak of war between Iran and Iraq leading to further OPEC increases. By 1980 the price per barrel had risen to $41. For companies, that was the good news; the bad news was that states were now in charge. Not only was OPEC dictating the price of oil, but for the most part, oil producing states spent the early 1970s nationalizing their petroleum industries and taking direct control of development and production. Private companies had fewer opportunities to develop and sell their own petroleum resources; the North Sea was a rare opportunity. Everyone wanted in on the action.

Setting the Foundation

The Norwegians, particularly officials in the executive bureaucracy, were looking for opportunities to increase state involvement offshore. In 1970, as the magnitude of the Ekofisk discovery became apparent to both state and industry officials (Ekofisk was not officially declared commercial until January 1971), the government launched several studies aimed at reforming the offshore system. The first Ministry of Industry (Norway), *Report No. 76* (30 April 1971) focused on restructuring the state institutions required to make and implement petroleum policy. It was deeply influenced by an Iraqi geologist named Farouk Al-Kasim, who in 1968 moved to Oslo with his Norwegian wife and disabled son. Al-Kasim had witnessed how IOCs had exploited Middle Eastern oil riches, returning little to the host states, and was determined to do what he could to prevent Norway from becoming another victim of resource exploitation. Working initially as a geologist, Al-Kasim later advised the Ministry of Industry in its writing of this first report on Norwegian oil management. The paper reflected Al-Kasim's perspective: Norway should reject the North American system that allowed IOCs to reap most of the offshore profits and ensure that petroleum production on the NCS benefited Norwegian society. At the heart of the report was a push for an expansive role for the Norwegian state. Norway had to have full control over activities on the NCS, while preserving private sector competition. The report also advocated high offshore tax rates and the establishment of a state-owned petroleum company (Tonstad and Al-Kasim, 2023, Chapters 6–7).[9]

---

[9]   As head of resources management in the new Norwegian Petroleum Directorate, Al-Kasim had opportunity to implement these recommendations from 1972 to 1990 (Tonstad and Al-Kasim, 2023).

In a second study, the Petroleum Council, at the behest of the Ministry of Industry, examined the existing licensing system and proposed reforms. Moreover, just before the reforms came up for a vote in the Storting in June 1972, Parliament adopted a set of principles – later dubbed the 'Ten Oil Commandments' – to guide subsequent decisions. The principles, which were laid out in a White Paper written by the Standing Committee on Industry (Storting, 1971) sent a clear message that echoed the words of Johan Castberg 60 years earlier: the state would guarantee that petroleum production would 'benefit the entire nation' by being deeply involved in the entire process:

1. National supervision and control must be ensured for all operations on the NCS.
2. Petroleum discoveries must be exploited in a way which makes Norway as independent as possible of others for its supplies of crude oil.
3. New industry will be developed based on petroleum.
4. The development of an oil industry must take necessary account of existing industrial activities and the protection of nature and the environment.
5. Flaring of exploitable gas on the NCS must not be accepted except during brief periods of testing.
6. Petroleum from the NCS must as a general rule be landed in Norway, except in those cases where socio-political considerations dictate a different solution.
7. The state must become involved at all appropriate levels and contribute to a coordination of Norwegian interests in Norway's petroleum industry as well as the creation of an integrated oil community which sets its sights both nationally and internationally.
8. A state oil company will be established which can look after the government's commercial interests and pursue appropriate collaboration with domestic and foreign oil interests.
9. A pattern of activities must be selected north of the 62nd parallel which reflects the special socio-political conditions prevailing in that part of the country.
10. Large Norwegian petroleum discoveries could present new tasks for Norway's foreign policy.

By the end of 1972, the Storting had debated and passed significant offshore reforms. The process revealed little disagreement between the political parties over the broad outline of Norwegian petroleum policy. The entire process, however, took place largely beneath the public's radar. Norway, throughout this period, was busy tearing itself apart over European Community membership (in the end deciding not to join). Oil policy could not compete with questions of identity, so the public took little notice of the transformation offshore.

The push for reform in the UK came not from the state bureaucracy, but from the politicians. The discovery of oil in the Norwegian sector prompted the new Conservative government of Edward Heath to hold a fourth licensing round (a small Third Round had been held in 1970) to accommodate oil company interest in blocks further north near the Norwegian border. The Ministry's license criteria made no mention of participation by state-owned companies, but the Ministry did announce its intention to auction off several blocks. Altogether, 31 bids were received for the 15 blocks, with winning bids providing £37 million of government revenue. In comparison, the other 267 blocks only realized revenue of £2.7 million (Sunnevåg, 2000, p. 5). The auction revenue of £37 million into the Treasury ignited a political storm over whether British governments had been involved in a giant offshore giveaway to the companies (Kretzer, 1993; Sunnevåg, 2000). Kenneth Dam (1976, p. 39) concluded that the 'discretionary system turned out to be the most expensive subsidy'. Others argued that Dam's analysis failed to incorporate income from resource rent tax and other special taxation. In their view, it was possible to conclude only that bidding provided greater 'up front' revenue, an expected outcome from the auctioning of petroleum licenses.

The Conservative Heath government's experiment with a more market-oriented, North American approach did not go further. Soon a new Labour government took office eager to replicate Norwegian reforms.

Licensing

In the early 1970s, both the British and Norwegian governments implemented similarly statist approaches to petroleum licensing. Both rejected (at least for a time) a market-based auction approach to granting access to petroleum resources and embraced a discretionary system that distributed licenses through the application of administratively or politically established criteria (Taverne, 1999). These discretionary systems enabled the governments to define a set of legal conditions to which the participating companies were expected to conform (Davis, 2004, p. 5). The major advantage of such systems was that they provided the states with maximum flexibility in awarding licenses. By setting predetermined criteria, including work program commitments (Frewer, 2000; Hunter, 2015), technical, financial, and management standards (Bunter, 2002), and government access to geological information, the states were able to regulate the level of activity on the continental shelf and increase their access to specialized knowledge and expertise. Moreover, the systems allowed the states to favor some companies over others based on qualifications – or national origin. Cash bidding for licenses could raise money for cash-strapped governments, but states would give up much of their control. Britain and Norway in the 1970s preferred control.

Norway

Both countries sought greater influence over offshore activities primarily through increased state participation (see below), but they also tightened their licensing systems in important ways (see Table 2.3). In Norway, the Storting's flurry of activity in 1972 included the reorganization of the institutional framework governing the NCS. Responsibility for gathering geological data, offering technical advice to the Ministry, working with companies on every phase of production, and ensuring the companies carried out the Ministry's wishes fell to a new Norwegian Petroleum Directorate (NPD). Responsibility for policy making and implementation – including management of the licensing rounds – fell to a new Petroleum and Mining Department of the Ministry of Industry, which was made an independent Ministry of Petroleum and Energy (MPE) in 1978. In addition, the Storting fortified the licensing system. The basic structure – the size of the blocks, the types of licenses offered, its discretionary nature – remained intact. But the conditions were stricter: production licenses were shortened to 6+30 rather than 6+40 years, with 50 percent relinquished after six years (a one-step not two-step process); rental fees for blocks increased almost seven-fold and remained steeply progressive; royalty payments on oil were also made progressive; and the price of gas was linked directly to the market price of oil. These changes were designed to speed exploration and development of offshore resources while capturing for the state a larger portion of the economic rent that would otherwise go to the companies.

The Norwegian government was eager to intervene beyond the licensing system. In February 1974, the Ministry of Finance in the minority Labor government led by Trygve Bratteli issued *Parliamentary Report No. 25 (1973–74) Petroleum Industry in Norwegian Society (Report No. 25)* (Ministry of Finance, 1973–74). The report – which was started under the previous government but bore a distinct Labour mark – was the government's response to a political row in early 1973 over the 'landing' of oil and gas from Ekofisk. The geographical position of the giant field made transporting petroleum from Ekofisk to Norway inconvenient and hugely expensive. Thus, Phillips and the Storting agreed that the best solution was to land the gas via subsea pipeline to Emden, West Germany, and the oil via subsea pipeline to Teesside, England. Opposition arose immediately. Oil Commandment 6 stated clearly that, 'Petroleum from the NCS must as a general rule be landed in Norway... .' Many feared that this was the beginning of Norway's loss of control of activities offshore to outside pressures. The Norwegian public had just rejected European Community membership, but some felt that Europe was still intent on controlling the life blood of the national economy (Nelsen, 1991, p. 39). On the other side of the issue, the companies complained that the government had yet to determine an overall strategy for developing its offshore resources. The

Table 2.3   *The second licensing systems*

	Britain	Norway
Institutional Structure		
Cabinet Ministry	Department of Energy	Ministry of Petroleum & Energy
Administrative Agency		Norwegian Petroleum Directorate
State Oil Company	British National Oil Corporation	Statoil (Equinor)
Terms		
Block Size	250. sq. km	500 sq. km
Types of Licenses	• Exploration • Production	• Reconnaissance • Production
Length of Prod. License	6+40 yrs.	6+30 yrs.
Relinquishment Requirement	50% after 6 yrs.	50% after 6 yrs.
Fees	Progressive	Progressive
Work Program	Yes	Yes
State Participation	51% carried interest	20–50% carried interest
Allocation Method	Discretionary	Discretionary
Depletion		
Depletion Goals	Speedy exploitation of the UKCS	A 'moderate' rate of extraction
Depletion Authority	Ultimate power over production vested in the Sec. of State	Ultimate power over production vested in the minster
Taxes		
Royalties	12.5%	Oil: 8.6% Gas: 12.5%
Taxes	PRT+Corporate	ST+Corporate

Source: Nelsen (1991, pp. 36, 42). Used by permission.

result of this pressure was *Report No. 25* (1973–74) which represented a broad consensus across major interests and political parties. It also bore all the marks of Nordic social planning.

The central theme of *Report No. 25* was state control. The offshore system, it asserted, 'must provide Norwegian authorities with full control of all stages

in the operation: exploration, production, processing, export and marketing'
(1973–74, p. 9). The government would participate directly in offshore activities, but private companies would also play a prominent role – at least for
a time. 'In the long run', the report argued, 'full control of operations may be
secured, so that the State has full charge of all rights and obligations, allowing
the companies to operate under different forms of entrepreneur contracts'
(1973–74, p. 17). Clearly Norwegian officials had understood the changed
relationship between producer states and oil companies globally. They knew
states were now in charge.

The Norwegian state reserved the right to control every aspect of offshore
activity. What concerned the petroleum companies most, however, was the
state's intent to regulate the rate of depletion, i.e., the speed at which companies would be allowed to produce and sell petroleum. Companies understood
that state officials could use the licensing system to regulate the amount of
oil and gas produced through the frequency and size of the licensing rounds.
While the companies were always encouraging the state to offer more and
more attractive blocks, they were comfortable with the use of licensing to slow
or speed the rate of petroleum extraction through field development. What
they did not want to see was state officials regulating the rate of extraction
once fields were developed. Offshore consortia looked for a certain return on
their massive investments in North Sea development. If state officials had the
power to slow the rate of depletion *after* a field began production, companies
might not be able to service their debts causing (especially small companies)
real difficulties. Thus, companies resisted post-development state control.
Report No. 25, however, advocated 'a moderate rate of extraction', assumed to
mean about 90 Mtoe per year. Objections to this suggested rate of extraction
came from the right – the Conservative party and the anti-tax Anders Langes
Party – which thought the rate too slow (and the powers of the state too great)
and from the left (including groups representing fishing, agriculture, small
business, and the environment), which feared economic distortions and environmental damage caused by too rapid an extraction rate. The government,
however, remained committed to a moderate rate regulated primarily through
the licensing system but backed by an explicit right to limit production in the
national interest.

In practice, the use of licensing to control depletion proved a blunt instrument. The Ministry announced the Third Round in June 1973; only 32 blocks
were offered, with 20 eventually awarded, but dribbled out over five years
with eight in 1974, seven in 1976, four in 1977, and one in 1978. Exploration
resulted in no major finds, which threatened the survival of Norwegian
offshore suppliers. In response, the Ministry conducted a Fourth Round and
awarded eight blocks in 1979. These proved highly productive yielding four
commercial oil fields – Oseberg, Veslefrikk, Snorre, and Brage – and the

world's largest offshore gas field, Troll. With licensing proving to be an ineffective way of regulating production, the Ministry announced it would hold smaller rounds at regular intervals but use its power to delay production or modify a field's production plan to control depletion.

During this period, the Ministry also proceeded slowly and deliberately to open areas north of 62° N, the northern boundary of the North Sea. Companies had been pressuring the government to open northern areas since 1970 when they analyzed the results of seismic surveys. Northern coastal regions stood to benefit from offshore activity, but fishing and environmental groups opposed expansion. Environmental groups opposed drilling in the north on ideological grounds, but fishing groups (and the Ministry of Fisheries) could be placated if their demands for protected spawning and fishing grounds – and their demand that companies clean up the seabed after drilling operations – were met. Further complicating the issue was a drilling disaster on Ekofisk Bravo (Block 2/4) when a safety lapse in April 1977 led to an eight-day uncontrolled blowout. The Ministry reacted by further delaying drilling in the north. In 1979, the MPE issued a report detailing new environmental rules, regulations, and compensation requirements for the fishing industry, and a promise to 'ensure full national freedom of action with regard to timing and volume of production' (Noreng, 1980, p. 50). The fifth licensing round was conducted in 1979–80 with the first northern blocks awarded in early 1980.

A potential setback came in March 1980 when an accommodation platform, the *Alexander Kielland*, capsized in a storm killing 123 men. Groups immediately called on the MPE to halt exploration in the North, but the Ministry withstood the pressure and exploration continued. Both the Ekofisk Bravo blowout in 1977 and the *Alexander Kielland* capsize in 1980, however, brought into sharp focus offshore petroleum safety.

Britain
In Britain, politics pushed the government to reform offshore policy. Labour voices in Parliament attacked the Heath government for underestimating prospects on the UKCS – where drillers had just discovered oil giants Forties (1970) and Brent (1971) – and failing to secure Britain's fair share of the petroleum profits. The result was a bipartisan report issued by the PAC in February 1973. The *PAC Report* criticized the licensing terms offered in the Fourth Round as far too lenient in light of the changes in the international petroleum system and suggested that the discretionary system could be enhanced by some form of auction. Both parties agreed that changes were due, but they went into the February 1974 General Election advocating different approaches to reform. The Conservatives called for a strengthened tax system that would capture more of the offshore profits for the state while continuing to promote rapid development of petroleum resources and give the energy administra-

tion cabinet rank by creating a Department of Energy (DoE), which it did in January 1974. Labour, on the other hand, argued for a Norwegian model that substantially increased the state's control of offshore activities through tax reform, state participation, and the creation of a state-owned offshore corporation. Labour won.

The Labour government of Harold Wilson immediately reviewed offshore policy and issued a White Paper in July 1974 that called for a tax on petroleum profits, majority state participation in new licenses, a majority stake in existing licenses, the creation of a state oil company, and the power to control the level of production. The October 1974 General Election was fought on this policy agenda, while the Tories campaigned in favor of higher taxes and more thorough offshore regulation, but against state participation. Again, Labour won. This time the government put its policy proposals into legislation known as the *Petroleum and Submarine Pipe-Line Act 1975*. The Act dealt primarily with state participation, but it did require companies to solicit DoE approval for a field's overall production plan, as well as 'consent' to produce according to that plan for a specified period of time (usually two to five years). Such a system allowed state officials to monitor field production to hold companies accountable to 'good oil field practice'. But it also offered state officials a tool to control depletion rates in the 'national interest'. Most economists advocated a hands-off approach to production levels, for balance of payments reasons, as did the powerful United Kingdom Offshore Operators Association (UKOOA), which argued that market signals and the engineering demands of the oil fields were better criteria for setting depletion rates. But other voices from both political parties expressed a desire to hold production back. Some were worried about energy supplies during possible future OPEC embargoes, others worried that Britain's steep oil production curve was hastening the day when the UK would 'run out of oil', while still others thought oil prices would keep on rising making it financially prudent to keep oil appreciating in the ground (Nelsen, 1991, pp. 68–69). Labour, in the end, chose to placate the companies by promising not to cut production before 1982 on fields found before 1976, the so-called 'Varley Assurances'.[10] Britain chose to control production in principle but not in practice.

The 1975 Act did not alter the British licensing system (see Table 2.4). New terms were announced in 1976 in preparation for the Fifth Round. Officials made several changes to bring requirements more in line with the Norwegian model and to speed development. Licensees, for instance, were required to

---

[10]   The 'Varley Assurances' took their name from Secretary of State for Energy Eric Varley who promised the government would not order depletion cuts before 1982 on fields discovered before 1976.

Table 2.4   *The new licensing terms in practice*

	Britain	Norway
Block Size	250 sq. km	500 sq. km
Types of Licenses	• Exploration • Production	• Reconnaissance • Production
Length of Production License	7+30 yrs	6+30 yrs
Relinquishment Requirement	67% after 7 yrs	50% after 6 yrs
Fees	Progressive	Progressive
Work Program	Yes	Yes
State Participation	51%	• At least 50% on carried interest basis • Sliding Scale applied after declaration of commerciality
Allocation Method	Discretionary	Discretionary
Tools to Control Depletion	approval of production program	• approval of production program • control over timing of field development
Depletion Policy in Practice	Varley Assurances prohibited production cuts	• reduced allocation of territory • explicit use of licensing rounds (later abolished)

Source: Nelsen (1991, pp. 60–61). Used by permission.

relinquish two-thirds of their license after seven years (not six); licensees would then receive a 30- (not 40)-year extension. Fees, as you would expect, rose dramatically, and became more progressive; and slight changes to the royalty system favored the state. The number of blocks on offer was the lowest yet (71), but the DoE was not using the round to slow production but rather to cool the overheated offshore supply sector that was contributing to construction delays and cost overruns.

Participation

The reform of the North Sea system in the early 1970s would have scarcely registered if changes in the licensing systems headlined the process. Such regulatory changes would be expected after significant discoveries 'proved' a new petroleum province. Reform, however, went much further during this period in both Britain and Norway for at the heart of the transformation of the policy regime was a decision by each state to engage in offshore activities, to take an active, ownership role in the development of petroleum resources on their continental shelves. Both states became oil entrepreneurs.

Norway
In Norway, the Storting voted unanimously in June 1972 to establish a brand new, fully integrated, completely state-owned oil company to manage the state's interest in offshore production licenses. There was some debate. The political right generally favored Norway's largest company, Norsk Hydro, as the best vehicle for the state's offshore interests, since it was already 51 percent state owned and well established in several industrial sectors. But the Storting decided that a new company would be best suited to 'take an active part in and have direct influence upon the management of all stages of operations', thus gaining 'effective control over activities on the continental shelf...' (Ministry of Industry (Norway), *Storting Proposition,* 2 February 1973, p. 21). On 18 September 1972, the Norwegian state created Den norske stats olje-selskap A/S, known as Statoil. The Minister of Industry was designated the company's 'general assembly' – its sole shareholder – thus placing it under political control.

Norwegian authorities in the second licensing round had introduced state participation, which could come in two forms, profit-sharing and carried interest. Profit-sharing did not allow state control of the field development process and was dropped as an option in subsequent rounds. That left 'carried interest' as the characteristic form of state participation on the NCS (see Table 2.4). Under this system, the state awarded itself (i.e., Statoil) an interest between 20 and 50 percent of each license. Private companies in the consortium then 'carried' Statoil's share of the costs through the exploration phase but included the company in all aspects of the operation. If the venture discovered a commercially viable field, Statoil chose to either proceed with development and share costs from that time forward or withdraw from the consortium. Statoil also had the right to participate in any downstream projects, such as pipelines and refineries. Thus, in quick order, the Norwegian state, through Statoil, gained access to all available information on the continental shelf, participated in all decisions concerning petroleum recovery, reaped its share of the profits – and bore little to none of the financial risk. The Norwegian state had won a sweet deal for its citizens – and it promised to use the bounty, as *Report No. 25* put it, to shape a 'qualitatively better society' (1973–74, pp. 6–7).

Britain
Political, economic, and social interests united in Norway behind state control of offshore activities through a state-owned company. Not so in Britain. British parties were divided over the issue forcing voters to decide the role of the state offshore.

The Conservative and Labour parties both favored greater state control of activities on the UKCS. They differed, however, on whether that increased control required state ownership of a petroleum company. The Conservatives argued that a new regulatory agency modelled on the NPD combined with an effective tax regime was all the state needed to control offshore activity and recover economic rent. The creation of a British National Oil Corporation (BNOC) and state participation struck Tories as purely ideological, a bow to Socialism. Labour, on the other hand, argued that Britain needed a state oil company to manage the state's participation interests, explore for petroleum, buy and sell oil and gas, trade in petroleum products, and build and operate refineries, pipelines, and tankers in the nation's interest. BNOC, in Labour's view, was to be an instrument of government policy as well as a commercial enterprise. Moreover, BNOC profits and the government's royalty collections were to be paid into a National Oil Account (NOA), from which the company would borrow (with the secretary of state's permission) the funds it needed for offshore operations, thus freeing the Treasury from offshore liabilities. The Conservatives, of course, found such an arrangement unattractive, unnecessary, and inherently contradictory as BNOC's commercial interests collided with its role as policy instrument. Nevertheless, Parliament's passage of the *Petroleum and Submarine Pipe-Line Act* (PSPLA) birthed BNOC on 1 January 1976.

One of the most controversial aspects of the PSPLA was the requirement that existing licenses be revised to grant the state at least a 51 percent share. The companies resisted the retroactive nature of the new policy. Initially this revision was presented as 'voluntary', but eventually the companies agreed to talks with the Ministry. The DoE first targeted companies in financial difficulty or in need of a government favor. The price of state assistance was relinquishment of a controlling share of the license to BNOC. The larger companies, after protracted negotiations and veiled DoE threats of exclusion in future licensing rounds, eventually agreed to what amounted to oil purchasing contracts rather than ownership arrangements. BNOC thus acquired a 51 percent share in the consortia, entitling it to a seat at the table and a vote (but not a veto) on the operating committees. It also entitled the company to 51 percent of the oil produced from fields that were only just coming online from the early discoveries, which BNOC would buy and (usually) immediately sell back to the consortia partners at the same price, provided there was no national emergency. In owning this majority stake, BNOC gained access to the inner workings of the operating consortia, but just as importantly, it became a major oil trading company as oil fields began to produce.

New licenses, those issued beginning with the Fifth Round in 1976–77, required BNOC to hold at least a 51 percent share of all licenses. The British, however, did not implement a full Norway-style carried interest system (see Table 2.4). BNOC paid its full share of the exploration costs like other partners. It did, however, require its partners to 'carry' it through the expensive development phase, in effect forcing them to make loans to the state company until the field began producing for the market. Thus, not unexpectedly, the British state with its overriding goal of speedy development, conceded a bit more ground on participation to the companies than did the Norwegian state. But all in all, the two countries took very similar approaches to state participation offshore.

Mercantilism

British and Norwegian politicians and state officials believed offshore activities would likely fuel an industrial and service sector bonanza that would bring high-paying jobs and new technologies to their economies. But such a result was not guaranteed. The oil giants came to the North Sea with management expertise and ready-made supply chains using proven suppliers and proprietary technologies. Government officials – explicitly in Norway, implicitly in the UK – recognized the need to disrupt traditional corporate relationships and direct as much offshore activity to domestic companies as possible. Both countries, therefore, adopted a mercantilist approach to petroleum development.

Norway

By 1975, Norway had developed a three-pronged strategy for maximizing the industrial benefits of offshore petroleum production. First, officials focused on increasing the equity shares and operator responsibilities of Norwegian petroleum companies, namely Statoil, Norsk Hydro, and Saga (a smaller, wholly private company created in 1972 at the direction of state authorities). Thus, in the Third Round of licensing (1974–78), Statoil was granted its controlling share in the 12 licenses awarded, while Norsk Hydro and Saga gained representation in a total of seven licenses. The roles of 'operator', or leading partner, of each license went to Statoil (4), Norsk Hydro (3), and Saga (1), with four going to non-Norwegian firms. A special allocation of a 'golden block' went to an all-Norwegian consortium with Esso serving as a technical advisor, which caused some foreign firms to wonder if they were now relegated to petroleum consulting. The Fourth Round (1979) proved that was not the case as each Norwegian company was appointed an operator on an attractive license, but no license went to a consortium comprised exclusively of Norwegian companies.

Second, officials used the unofficial bidding process for licenses to encourage commitments to use Norwegian offshore goods and services companies. A 1972 law[11] required operators to use Norwegian suppliers when they were competitive on quality, service, delivery time, and price and to open

---

[11]   *Royal Decree of Dec. 8, 1972, Relating to Exploration for and Exploitation of Petroleum in the Seabed and Substrata of the Norwegian Continental Shelf.*

the bidding process to government scrutiny (Tønne, 1983). Authorities also made it clear that a company's record of awarding contracts to Norwegian firms would be considered when allocating licenses. During this period, the award of goods and services contracts favored the Norwegian applicant because a Norwegian tender was calculated as value added (in manpower and monetary terms). A Norwegian tender could be up to 10 percent higher than the lowest bid and still win the contract (Noreng, 2004). Thus, by 1978, the Norwegian share of offshore business rose to 62 percent from 28 percent in 1975. Norwegian officials also scrutinized exploration and development plans for their commitments to training Norwegian personnel, locating research and development in Norway (Colombia Centre on Sustainable Investment, 2016).

Finally, Norwegian authorities encouraged foreign petroleum companies to assist in the general development of Norwegian industry through technology transfers, the use of domestic research and development, and investment in non-petroleum-related projects. Companies, especially in the Fifth Round, tried to impress officials with promises of millions of dollars for industrial projects that were never subjected to cost-benefit screening. Many of the projects, therefore, were criticized as ill-conceived (Sampson, 1975, pp. 314–315).

Britain

Norwegian energy policy explicitly set as a goal the Norwegianization of the NCS. Britain did not adopt such a policy as part of its offshore strategy, but developed an independent Britainization policy that achieved similar results. Britain's membership in the European Community, which discouraged national favoritism, and the fact that much of the UKCS had already been licensed made allocating licenses to British petroleum companies more difficult than in Norway. Of course, BNOC received its majority share of the licenses allocated in the Fifth (1976–77) and Sixth Rounds (1978–79), but the DoE also selected BNOC as the operator for ten attractive blocks with other operatorships going to several private (UK) companies. Furthermore, if any company awarded a share of licenses allocated in Rounds 1–4 decided to relinquish its share, BNOC would have the right of first refusal. Finally, the DoE exercised its right to allocate blocks to state companies outside of the regular rounds and awarded nine exclusive licenses to BNOC and one to the British Gas Corporation (BGC) in spring 1978. Thus, the DoE successfully raised the state's (and overall British) ownership and control of offshore assets by exercising what powers it had to favor UK petroleum companies.

As for the offshore supply market, the British state took a particularly aggressive approach to promote British interests which had begun during the Conservative Heath government. An independent report issued early in 1973 pointed to massive problems in the British supplies industry that threatened to shut UK industry out of its own offshore market (Nelsen, 1991, p. 74).

In response, the Heath government established an Offshore Supplies Office (OSO), introduced a process for thoroughly auditing petroleum company purchases, and provided financial assistance to the offshore goods and services industry. The OSO was given extensive powers to review purchasing plans and bidding procedures and used its close contact with offshore operators and its power to publicly shame companies to push them towards buying British. When Labour came to power in 1974, the new government expanded the size of the OSO and worked to market British products and support British research and development. In addition, the DoE negotiated a Memorandum of Understanding with UKOOA that gave the OSO the right to review lists of companies invited to bid on projects (and add names if necessary) and to examine the bids. Final decisions were up to the operators, but all knew that the use of British suppliers would be a factor in the awarding of future licenses. By the end of the 1970s, Britain too had raised domestic shares of the offshore market to over 60 percent.

By the close of the 1970s, Britain and Norway had successfully shifted offshore operations toward national enterprises. The most visible beneficiaries – and symbols of the new nationalistic offshore policies – were the national petroleum companies, BNOC and Statoil. Both companies grew rapidly in size and power: Statoil took at least a 50 percent stake in every license issued after 1972, served as operator of promising projects, participated as an observer in licensing negotiations between the MPE and other petroleum companies, and advised the Ministry and NPD as a quasi-governmental agency; BNOC received controlling shares of new licenses, but also took over the offshore assets and technical teams of the National Coal Board (which had stakes in five oil and four gas fields) and the offshore assets and related personnel of struggling Burmah Oil. Both of these companies expanded very quickly in terms of territory, personnel, information, expertise, and financial clout. They became significant players in the North Sea virtually overnight.

Opposition

By design, both BNOC and Statoil were on short political leashes. Statoil's supreme authority was the minister who was responsible to the Storting. The company's articles of incorporation, however, required Statoil to seek the approval of Parliament for any action that could foreseeably impact the nation politically or economically. In practice, ministers felt an obligation to keep the Storting fully informed of every move Statoil planned, with many of the proposals debated on the floor of Parliament. BNOC was also controlled by the government through the Secretary of State for Energy, who with the Treasury, directly controlled the company's finances. Parliament received very little information from BNOC and did not exercise any more than perfunctory oversight.

Such rapid growth drew public scrutiny, and it did not take long in either country for opposition to grow. In Norway, the Center party questioned the ability of the MPE to effectively check Statoil and accused the Ministry of letting the company get away with making decisions without Storting input and vague statements about its future plans. Statoil, for its part, resisted offering the Storting access to information valued by its competitors on the NCS. In Britain, the Labour government took seriously BNOC's role as an instrument of industrial policy and ordered it to buy an oil rig from an ailing British shipyard. BNOC, for its part, found ways around some of the financial restrictions placed on it by the DoE and gained access to large sums of money by selling forward its crude oil. These actions raised serious objections. Opponents also questioned BNOC's influence over the licensing process: with its inside information and its direct contact with the DoE, BNOC seemed to direct its way operational responsibility for highly promising blocks (Nelsen, 1991, pp. 79–82).

Vocal opposition to the state companies soon emerged. Petroleum companies on both shelves complained about the state companies' arrogance and unfair advantages that undermined the spirit of competition and fair play. Conservative voices in both countries accused the left-wing governments of nationalizing the continental shelves and squeezing private companies out of the province. In Norway, Norsk Hydro organized a group of companies working on the NCS as an alternative source of advice to the Ministry on petroleum policy. In Britain, the private oil companies also resented the role of BNOC as operator, government spy, and quasi government agency. They were beginning to see the struggle with BNOC as an existential battle. The Conservative party under its new leader Margaret Thatcher was, more and more, inclined to agree.

Taxation

The discoveries in the North Sea, the dramatic rise in crude oil prices, and the fundamental shift in power away from the major oil companies to the host governments made it clear to both Norwegian and British politicians that the state was not recovering its share of offshore rents. The offshore tax regime needed drastic reform (see Table 2.3).

Both governments formulated new tax proposals at the end of 1974 and the two Parliaments passed them in 1975 after extensive consultations with the companies, and with each other (Morgan and Robinson, 1976). The central feature of each new regime was a new tax on petroleum profits. In Norway, the 'Special Tax' was set at 25 percent of net income from petroleum production and pipeline transport and was levied in addition to the standard corporate tax of 50.8 percent and the royalty requirements. To prevent price manipulation for tax purposes, the government established a Norwegian Petroleum Price Board that determined a quarterly 'norm price' (the average price of crude oil traded by independent entities in the free market) that would be used to calculate a company's Special Tax obligation. To soften the tax blow, the Norwegian law allowed companies to deduct from their reported income their petroleum-related expenditures from anywhere on the NCS and their royalty payments from their income calculated for corporate tax. They were also allowed – for 15 years – to deduct from their Special Tax 10 percent of the purchase value of their offshore installations and equipment (the so-called 'uplift' provision). These modifications of the system added a progressive element that encouraged companies to continue to invest at a high level in the NCS. In similar fashion, the British introduced a new Petroleum Revenue Tax (PRT) set at 45 percent, but also allowed a series of deductions, which included capital expenditures on the UKCS, an uplift of 75 percent deducted from the PRT (but for expenditures associated with only the corresponding field – the so-called 'ring fence'), and an 'oil allowance' of half a million tons of oil per six-month period that was also deducted from PRT. In addition, the legislation gave the Ministry the authority to defer royalty payments and institute safeguard measures if it deemed such measures necessary to the commercial viability of the field.

The tax laws adopted in 1975 raised the governments' 'take' from North Sea profits to approximately 70 percent, with the British taking a bit more than the Norwegians. The system remained stable until the late 1970s when another oil shock rocked the world.

Assessing the New Systems

The policy transformation of the 1970s resulted in both Britain and Norway adopting a *participatory* system – an interventionist regulatory structure coupled with a state-owned petroleum enterprise that managed the state's ownership interests and implemented government policy. Again, as in the early years, policy in Britain and Norway *converged* around a regional norm. The North Sea system was now participatory.

Our question is why? What had changed?

First, the international petroleum system had fundamentally transformed during the infant period of North Sea petroleum development. Several system changes had strengthened the states in relation to the IOCs. Some of these changes were specific to the North Sea province and the individual littoral states. The North Sea, for instance, was a proven but still unexplored oil and gas province. Dramatically rising prices and the seizing of control of oil production by governments in the Middle East made finds in the North Sea commercially viable and the entire province highly desirable to private oil companies. In the meantime, Norway and the UK had recruited high-skilled individuals to aid in the accumulation of necessary knowledge, developed bureaucratic institutions to oversee offshore development, and instituted strict reporting requirements that allowed government decision makers to match the technical expertise and information resources of the companies at the bargaining table. Furthermore, each country had adopted a discretionary licensing system that ordered offshore competition and, just as important, gave state regulators a powerful tool (i.e., the prospect of future licenses) to control the behavior of IOCs. By 1974, this combination of national reform, combined with seismic shifts in the international supply of petroleum because of the 1973 oil embargo, meant that system conditions had shifted dramatically in favor of governments in oil producing provinces. This gave state agencies tremendous leverage at the petroleum level (see Figures 2.3 and 2.4).

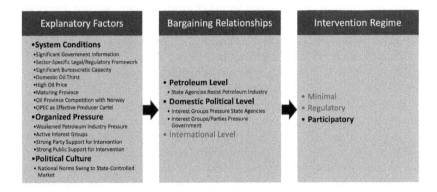

Figure 2.3   Transformation: Britain

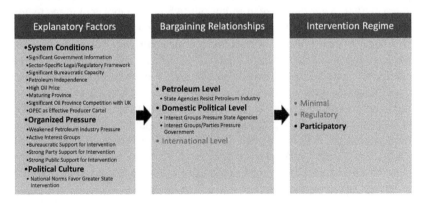

Figure 2.4   Transformation: Norway

Second, non-oil interest groups also took note of offshore oil policy, in part because domestic oil finds merited significant headlines, in part because European Community (EC) membership was no longer a topic of debate, especially in Norway. In the 1970s, interest organizations – from fishing, to the environment, to offshore supply associations – began pressing the governments for beneficial interventionist policies. Political parties – from both left and right, but most strongly from the left – advocated deeper and more visible state intervention on the continental shelf. And public opinion also came to favor more state involvement in the North Sea to counter the profit-hungry oil companies intent on stealing the offshore bonanza. These interests put pressure on governments to exert more control over development and production on the continental shelf – enough to counter the organized pressure of the offshore petroleum companies. The companies still had tremendous influence over the details of policy. But, try as they might, they had little power to thwart the main thrust of petroleum policy, which aimed at substantial government ownership of offshore resources, combined with massive state intervention in the search for and development, production, and sale of offshore oil and gas. Thus, in the 1970s, petroleum policy engaged not just the petroleum level, but the domestic political level as well. Here too the oil companies found themselves in a much weaker position vis-à-vis the domestic political parties and interest groups.

Both Britain and Norway responded to the changed systemic conditions and the rise of domestic politics by intervening in the North Sea, even to the point of creating their own fully integrated oil companies to get in on the offshore action. Even from this point of convergence, however, there were minor differences between the two countries' policies. Unlike Britain, Norway remained energy independent of the North Sea, requiring very little of what it produced to power the country. Consequently, Norway was less concerned about offering petroleum companies easier terms than Britain to maintain 'offshore market share'. Norwegian authorities, who were more committed to government intervention and more proactive in pursuing control than were their British counterparts, more successfully negotiated meaningful retroactive state participation in existing licenses than did the British, who essentially agreed to emergency access to oil. Norway also took a slower, more deliberate approach to offshore licensing and development, using this slower pace to develop and implement a coherent national policy that sought to place the Norwegian state at the center of petroleum development, and Norwegian industry and society as recipients of the benefits of such development. Norwegian officials certainly understood the need to develop fields at a technically responsible pace, but they were also aware that the country could afford to take its time issuing licenses to its vast offshore territory. The UK on the other hand, remained hungry for domestic oil and oil profits; speedy development of newly discovered offshore fields remained its top priority. This gave the UK sector a frenetic feel that never quite characterized the Norwegian sector. In addition, the two countries still had different political cultures: the British were more comfortable with feverish competition among mostly private enterprises, while the Norwegians were more comfortable with controlled capitalism. These political cultures were woven into the fabrics of the two countries' offshore policies.

The differences were real, but the remarkable characteristic of offshore policies in Norway and Britain in the 1970s was their underlying similarity. The two countries had converged on a participatory offshore regime that brought in vast wealth to their respective treasuries without disastrously dampening company enthusiasm for a piece of the North Sea action. Changes, however, were afoot. As the 1970s gave way to the 1980s, Margaret Thatcher shook up the ideological consensus of the postwar period. The rise of Thatcherism set the scene for policy divergence offshore.

3. Divergence: checking state ownership and control

The United Kingdom (UK) and Norway established remarkably similar offshore systems in the 1960s and 1970s. But that changed in the 1980s as the Norwegian state exercised greater authority over the pace of offshore development and the rate of production on some fields, whereas Britain sold the British National Oil Corporation (BNOC) and exited the offshore sector as a business participant. Thus, as we shall see, after a brief experiment with participatory intervention, the British settled back on regulatory intervention while Norway strengthened its participatory system. This policy divergence reflected different levels of social comfort with government participation in the market, which, in turn, reflected differing political cultures. The Norwegians clearly felt more at home with a statist approach that embraced a state-market balance tipped toward the state; the British were more liberal and, thus, reluctant to give the state too much influence over economic decisions best left to the market (Taylor and Soliman Hunter, 2019, pp. 57–58). Policy divergence in the 1980s must be understood in light of these differences in political culture, but also as the product of a changed domestic and international context. That is where we start this chapter.

CONTEXT

Labour governments in the 1970s in Britain and Norway presided over difficult economic times. Growth stagnation, rapid inflation, currency instability, and rising debt plagued both countries – a pattern that fit most of the western industrialized democracies at this time (Kopp, 2015). The collapse of the Bretton Woods international monetary system, the oil embargo of 1973, and the rise of industrial competition from countries in the Global South, particularly in steel production, contributed to a period of 'stagflation' in the West,[1] where slow economic growth and rapidly rising prices created what had been thought to be impossible, high unemployment with simultaneous inflation.

---

[1] A term coined in 1965 by Iain Macleod, Conservative politician, and Chancellor of the Exchequer, appointed one month before his death in 1970.

British Labour felt the political ramifications first. Bitter strikes and the breakdown in some government services in 1978–79 (often called the 'Winter of Discontent') led to a successful parliamentary vote of no confidence in James Callaghan's Labour government. A general election followed and the Conservative party, led by Margaret Thatcher, won a clear victory. Across the North Sea, the Norwegian Labour party faced the same political discontent, losing ten seats in the Storting elections of 1981. The Norwegian Conservative party benefited most from Labour's defeat and formed a minority government, which Prime Minister Kåre Willoch transformed in 1983 into a majority center-right coalition, the first majority nonsocialist government since the end of World War II. Thus, both electorates reacted to economic trouble by replacing socialists with conservatives in government.

While the Conservative-led government in Norway was considered friendlier to business, it could hardly be described as radical. The presence of the Christian Democrats and Center party in the coalition ensured a pull to the center. The Thatcher government in Britain was a different story. The Tory soul-searching that followed the disastrous Heath government and two 1974 election defeats opened the door to new thinking on economic governance. Standard Tory support for government involvement in the economy gave way to a more classically liberal, anti-government, pro-market perspective heavily influenced by Friedrich Hayek, Milton Friedman, and Margaret Thatcher's intellectual guide, Sir Keith Joseph. Thatcher's team came into office committed to shrinking the public sector and reducing regulation; it sought to solve Britain's economic problems by lifting from private enterprise the heavy hand of government, thereby enabling the 'invisible hand' of self-interest operating in a free-market to realize wealth-creating efficiencies. The party committed to selling some or all state shares in a few important companies, including British Petroleum (BP), which the Labour government commenced selling in 1977 and the Tories completed in 1987 (Hoopes, 1997). But BP was not one of the government's primary instruments of control offshore. That designation belonged to BNOC, and the Conservatives initially tread lightly. In the 1979 election campaign, the Tories promised only to examine the role of BNOC and promote Britain's energy flexibility. But no one doubted that Britain's new Labour-inspired offshore system of participatory intervention might eventually become a target of Thatcher's government.

In addition to domestic political changes in both countries, shifting international relations and changes in global petroleum markets also posed challenges to the North Sea system (see Thompson, 2022). As we saw in the previous chapter, Arab-Israeli conflict in the Middle East, a wave of nationalizations of foreign oil companies, and the new assertiveness of the Organization of Petroleum Exporting Countries (OPEC) inspired an unprecedent level of conflict between petroleum-producing countries (mostly in the Middle

East) and consuming countries (mostly in the industrialized West). Britain and Norway found themselves caught in the middle; they were petroleum producers with petroleum-consuming allies. Britain, unsurprisingly, had less trouble than Norway toeing the Western alliance's political line. The nation had played a leading role in the intellectual and institutional development of Europe and had remained a great European and global imperial power for over two centuries. Exporting petroleum was not going to alter Britain's basic international orientation. Thus, when the United States (US) called the petroleum-consuming countries together in 1974 to form the International Energy Agency (IEA) as a counter to OPEC, the British agreed to charter membership with its commitment to participate in an emergency oil-sharing plan in the event of a crisis. Britain did not, however, extend its willingness to share its petroleum resources beyond emergency situations, even with its European Community (EC) partners. When a member of the EC Commission suggested that Britain's oil was a 'Community resource' to be shared, British politicians reacted with predictable ire (Shackleton, 1978).

Norway's international position was more complicated than Britain's. It was certainly a pillar of the Western alliance as a charter member of the North American Treaty Organization (NATO), but Norway was also cognizant of its role as a traditional bridgebuilder between the rich West and the developing world, as well as wary of agreements that placed national decisions in the hands of supranational institutions. Thus, the decision to join the IEA – with its aggressive stance toward OPEC and its mandatory emergency oil-sharing provisions – proved tricky. The Labour government supported membership but faced domestic opposition, most importantly from within the Labour party itself. As a result, the government negotiated an agreement with the IEA that gave Norway full membership rights but allowed the country to preserve its options in an emergency by giving it the right to opt out of the oil-sharing plan. Norway joined the IEA in 1975, but not before toying briefly in late 1974 with the idea of joining OPEC. The government rejected the notion in early 1975, but nevertheless joined Britain in a series of high-level contacts with OPEC officials throughout the 1970s (Ausland, 1979; Noreng, 1979).

Norway entered the 1980s trying to remain on good terms with both petroleum consuming and producing countries. The low-profile strategy worked as long as the global energy 'players' took little notice. But geopolitical conflict and oil price volatility in the 1980s made Norway's position less tenable as pressures mounted to take sides in the struggle between producers and consumers. Britain was less concerned about maintaining a middle ground between the oil interests, but it too felt pressure on its North Sea policies as the 1980s wore on.

REGULATION

The rise of more conservative, business-friendly governments in Britain and Norway in the 1980s could have led to a predictable rollback of state regulation offshore. Deregulation, however, did not happen on either continental shelf. The right-wing governments in both countries accepted the basic offshore regulatory and institutional structures established by their left-wing opponents. Moreover, in Norway the center-right coalition actually continued the general expansion of state control of the offshore sector, as we will see below. In Britain, the Thatcher government held steady the regulatory regime, in part because the rules achieved important safety, security of supply, and industrial development goals, and in part because Conservatives saw effective regulation as the alternative to state participation offshore.

Licensing in both countries remained fundamentally unchanged, but both governments tinkered around the edges in response to interest group pressure and shifts in the oil market (see Table 3.1). In Britain, the Conservative government responded to pressure from the petroleum companies (via the United Kingdom Offshore Operators Association, UKOOA), the House Select Committee on Energy, and the French and German governments (which were concerned about the slow pace of development), by increasing the number of blocks made available for exploration. By continuing the Labour government's practice of conducting rounds on a regular two-year cycle, and by tripling the average number of blocks on offer per round, the Department of Energy (DoE) introduced a continuous licensing process, which pleased the oil companies but made it very difficult for fishing and environmental groups to mount enough pressure to block licensing in sensitive areas. Furthermore, during this time the DoE also sought to open new areas – for instance, to the west of Scotland and in northern waters near the Shetland Islands – by making it clear to companies that success in gaining acreage in proven areas depended on commitments to explore risky frontier blocks also. The strategy seemed to succeed when oil prices were relatively high, but when prices fell towards the end of the decade, market realities forced the DoE to remove the link between attractive and frontier blocks.

The British DoE continued to award most licenses on a discretionary basis, but in addition it also revived the practice of auctioning some blocks. It would be wrong, however, to attribute the change to the market ideology of the Thatcher government; auctioning blocks – which the oil companies opposed – seemed a sure revenue generator for the Treasury (Forster and Zillman, 1983). Thus, in the Seventh Round (1980–81) companies were allowed to nominate blocks in mature sectors for a fee of £5 million per block. The DoE awarded 42 blocks and collected £210 million – a successful result. The Eighth and

Table 3.1   Licensing terms in the 1980s

	Britain	Norway
Block Size	250 sq. km	500 sq. km
Types of Licenses	• Exploration • Production	• Reconnaissance • Production
Length of Production Licenses	6+40 yrs	6(+4)+30 yrs
Relinquishment Requirement	50% after 6 yrs	50% after 6 yrs
Fees	Progressive	Progressive
Work Program	Yes	Yes
State Participation	None*	• at least 50% on carried interest basis (until '87) • one-step sliding scale after declaration of commerciality
Application Method	By groups	Individually
Allocation Method	Discretionary/Auction	Discretionary

Note: *Officially, the state still 'participated' (without owning shares) through participation agreements managed by the Oil and Pipelines Agency (OPA).
Source: Nelsen (1991, p. 91). Used by permission.

Ninth rounds returned to a more traditional auction method, but only 15 blocks were offered for bid in each round, a mere eight percent of the total blocks opened. The Eighth Round raised only £33 million, but the more successful Ninth Round brought in £121 million. The weakening oil market and Treasury surpluses at the end of the 1980s made auctions less attractive. As a result, the DoE decided to conduct the final rounds of the decade (the Tenth and Eleventh) as pure discretionary rounds.

The Norwegian licensing system remained even more stable than the British, but not unchanged. The Willoch government recognized the value of keeping offshore investment within a certain range to avoid the economic trauma of boom-and-bust cycles (Dølvik and Oldervoll, 2019). The Ministry of Petroleum and Energy (MPE) thus began conducting nearly annual rounds, although the number of blocks offered seldom exceeded 15. The opening of offshore areas north of 62° N permitted the Ministry to focus much of its attention on unproven territory. Environmental and fishing interests (and the ministries that represented their interests in the government) still carried some clout with the MPE and blocked or delayed the awarding of some northern blocks, but the interests of the northern districts in the economic activity generated by offshore exploration and development overcame most of the barriers to northern licenses.

One element of the Norwegian licensing system made permanent during this period deviated from practice on the United Kingdom Continental Shelf (UKCS). The British encouraged groups of companies to apply for offshore blocks and the DoE awarded licenses to these consortia. Norwegian officials had always taken a more active role in forming the consortia holding the licenses. In 1985, the government formalized its role through a new *Petroleum Activities Act* that required companies to apply for blocks as single entities and to specify the proportion of the license it wanted to hold and whether it wished to be named operator. When making an award, the MPE then identified the companies (usually two to five) in the consortium, the percentage of shares they held, and which among them was named operator. The Norwegian government, thus, created the consortia operating on the Norwegian Continental Shelf (NCS) (see Table 3.1). In addition, the government required each party in a consortium to sign a Joint Operating Agreement (JOA), the terms of which were transparent and non-negotiable. The Norwegian state's active role in forming the consortia and naming the operators enabled the government to insert its interests into the consortia. It also offered the state an additional tool to promote Norwegian interests in technology transfer, research and development, and industrial expansion in the oil and gas sector.

Governments in both countries used their offshore licensing systems as instruments of industrial policy. The Thatcher government continued Labour's policy of favoring British companies when awarding licenses, but shifted its support away from state-owned to private enterprises. A host of companies without any competence in offshore petroleum activity joined consortia for speculative and tax-avoidance purposes, which annoyed the oil companies and led to some tightening of the system after 1983. The government, however, continued to encourage the smaller, independent (from the oil majors) British petroleum companies that flourished in the early 1980s. The fall in oil prices later in the decade forced a consolidation of the offshore sector, but it was generally acknowledged that the independent companies brought innovation and efficiency to the UKCS that raised overall production (Nelsen, 1991, pp. 98–99).

More controversial were successful efforts by Britain to capture the offshore goods and services market for British suppliers.[2] Again, using the licensing process, British officials encouraged companies to use domestic suppliers if they were 'competitive in regard to specification, service, delivery and price'

---

[2]   The British eventually controlled 90% of the offshore market.

(Nelsen, 1991, p. 100). Unofficially offshore operators committed to placing around 70 percent of their orders with British companies. Few companies chose to challenge the government on this protectionist policy. When they did, economic and political interests exerted withering pressure on the company to reverse the decision – which happened to Sun Oil in 1984 when it chose a Swedish company to build a floating production platform it needed on a tight time schedule. Most companies eventually buckled under pressure, but when Sun Oil resisted, the DoE excluded it from the subsequent licensing round as an example to the entire offshore sector. Britain's partners in the EC eventually filed a complaint with the Commission charging the British with discrimination against European suppliers. As a result, Britain dropped its intention to evaluate license applications on commitments to use British suppliers, but the issue did not go away.

In Norway, efforts to Norwegianize the NCS continued with the appointment of Statoil to most operatorships. But this did not lead to the exclusion of foreign companies from licensing rounds as some had hoped. Norwegian companies and government officials recognized the need for the experience and technical expertise only foreign companies could provide. The two Willoch governments of the early 1980s continued the practice of favoring the Norwegian trinity of Statoil, Norsk Hydro, and Saga. The Conservative party tended to favor the two private companies, Norsk Hydro and Saga; when the Christian People's party entered the government and took over the MPE, the private companies, which were more tied to urban interests than were the rural Christian Democrats, benefited less, while Statoil and European companies much more. Norwegian officials – unlike their British counterparts – did not allow the proliferation of small, independent petroleum companies on the NCS at this time. They preferred, instead, to award licenses to the trinity and a small group of trusted (mostly European) companies.

Norwegian offshore goods and services policy remained mercantilist, as it did in Britain. The *Petroleum Activities Act* gave officials the right to reject suppliers if they believed a Norwegian company better suited to get the contract, but in practice most of the pressure to buy Norwegian came through the discretionary licensing system. Companies knew that future licenses depended on their record of using Norwegian suppliers, which amounted to an informal protectionist policy. The policy, however, turned out to be a two-edged sword: the French held up a major gas deal until satisfied (informally) that Elf and Total (its major oil companies) would be offered attractive licenses and its suppliers would be favored during the development of the Troll field (Nelsen, 1991, p. 104). In addition, the center-right governments of the 1980s reaffirmed the policy of the 1970s that required petroleum companies to contribute to the overall industrial development of Norway. Many of these efforts remained inefficient and short-term. But the MPE, beginning with the

Fourth round, required companies to sign 'technology agreements' pledging to carry out as much petroleum-related research and development as possible in Norway in an effort to close the gap in technical expertise and know how.

During the 1980s, company and government officials began planning for the closure of offshore fields and the abandonment of production equipment. The complete removal of man-made structures was neither feasible nor even desirable in some cases. After much discussion with a broad range of interests, the British proposed a plan that received general acceptance. The plan called for a flexible regulation that required companies to remove equipment based on water depth: shallow fields required complete removal; deeper fields partial removal, or in rare cases, no removal. Furthermore, the government gained the right to hold parent companies – not just subsidiaries – responsible for decommissioning costs. The policy, which was set out in the UK's *Petroleum Act 1987*, proved controversial for its interventionist tone. The same policy in Norway, however, received no strong pushback by offshore companies accustomed to close Norwegian government oversight.

Finally, both Britain and Norway developed offshore oversight practices that allowed state officials to evaluate every aspect of field development and petroleum production. Participation agreements, of course, gave state officials access to the inner workings of the offshore consortia. But even as the British state pulled out as an owner and active investor on the UKCS, the DoE remained the final authority whose approval was necessary before projects could proceed. Oversight of the exploration, development, and production plans in Norway fell to the MPE and its regulatory agency, the Norwegian Petroleum Directorate (NPD), but the final authority remained the Storting. Unlike Britain, where approval was granted at Ministry level, the Norwegian Parliament approved every major offshore development. While discussions between British ministry officials and company representatives often centered around efficiency and 'good oil field practice', Storting members took up the interests of local communities eager for construction jobs or worried about fishing grounds. Parliamentary debates, therefore, quite often focused on the location of onshore facilities needed to service offshore platforms.

Both governments required license holders to issue reports on every aspect of offshore operations. Norwegian officials remained intent on issuing detailed regulations governing offshore safety and disaster prevention, which prompted some to complain that old rules were crowding out new safety procedures and technologies. Such detailed regulations were borne out of the Ekofisk Bravo blowout in 1977, and the *Alexander Kielland* flotel disaster three years later (see Chapter 2). The British government stuck to its self-regulation strategy, setting goals and letting companies find its own way to meet the standards. That changed when 167 men died in a natural gas explosion on the Piper field.

A series of additional accidents and heavy Labour union pressure forced the DoE to reexamine its safely policy.

Close government scrutiny made the regulatory weight on offshore companies immense. One Statoil official complained that the reporting requirements for a single North Sea platform exceeded one million documents costing $55–88 million (*Noroil Magazine*, 1988, p. 16). Safety concerns, however, were paramount and reporting requirements assured state agencies that they knew as much or more than the companies about petroleum sector threats to humans and the environment.

DEPLETION

Depletion policy, 'the regulation of petroleum production by the state according to some notion of what constitutes the ideal rate of extraction for the society' (Nelsen, 1991, p. 113), started the 1980s in the same place in Britain and Norway. But by the end of the decade the two countries had diverged markedly: the British state dropped any attempt to regulate production, while the Norwegian state refused to give up control. Maintaining control of depletion policy, however, made Norway vulnerable to international and domestic actors intent on influencing the volume of petroleum pumped from the NCS.

Britain

The British Conservatives came to power in 1979 in agreement with the previous Labour government on offshore depletion. Most Tories supported the state's right to regulate depletion, either through the field development process or via direct controls on production, but they were also committed to the Varley Assurances (see Chapter 2), which delayed any regulation until after 1982. Despite these assurances, the DoE announced in early 1981 that development of the new Clyde oil field would be delayed for two years. The reason, however, had nothing to do with oil depletion and everything to do with public sector spending. BNOC operated the Clyde field and would soon be required to pay its share of the field's development costs – approximately £350 million. The Treasury pressed for a five-year delay, but after consulting with the DoE and BNOC, settled for two years. That ended the only successful effort to manage industry production plans, and had nothing to do with managing production, and everything to do with delaying government spending. Eventually the Tories extended the government's promise not to intervene until 1985. When that deadline came and went without government comment, the issue faded from discussion.

Officially, Britain did not regulate the production of natural gas, but an unofficial policy in fact discouraged development of gas fields on the UKCS.

The British Gas Corporation (BGC) remained the monopsony buyer of British North Sea gas and used its position to keep prices low. Gas exports were prohibited, and only limited imports were allowed – just enough to keep downward pressure on prices and limit enthusiasm for exploration. BGC bought gas from Norway's declining Frigg field, and by the mid-1980s the British needed to find a replacement source. BGC and Statoil reached an agreement that would supply gas to Britain through 2010 from the new Sleipner field. The deal proved controversial. Eventually the Thatcher government, in a protectionist move, nixed the agreement due to Treasury concerns about the balance of payments and the loss of tax revenue to Norway. The decision ended the informal gas depletion policy and sparked new interest in the British gas sector, albeit still dampened by the prohibition against exports.

Norway

The 1980s brought an end to explicit state interference in offshore production in Britain. The same was not true in Norway. The Willoch government entered office in 1981 with Norway producing a little over 50 Mtoe of oil and gas. The Storting had set a 'moderate' production target of 90 Mtoe in the mid-1970s, but that goal was unattainable and clearly undesirable. Thus, the government appointed a royal commission in 1982 (the so-called Skånland Commission) to study the issue and make recommendations. The Commission eventually accepted the position taken most vocally by the NPD, which rejected production targets in favor of offshore investment goals. By controlling investment rather than production, the government would prevent the boom-bust cycle that so worried officials on both sides of the North Sea. It would also help placate the growing number of interest organizations representing groups with offshore economic interests – unions, offshore supply associations, coastal districts, and others. Steady investment, however, could see offshore production continue to climb flooding the economy with easy petrodollars. To prevent a dramatic distortion of the economy, in 1983, the Skånland Commission recommended the establishment of an oil fund to absorb excess income and invest it overseas where it would not affect the Norwegian economy.

The government accepted the recommendations of the Skånland Commission and began regulating offshore investment rather than production. (An oil glut, however, depressed prices in the last half of the 1980s forcing a delay in establishing the oil fund to 1990.) Problems, however, developed immediately. The only way to regulate investment was to delay some offshore projects, in effect establishing a field development 'queue'. MPE authorities and Storting members, therefore, opened themselves up to intense political pressure. Competition for 'queue slots' pitted offshore companies against one another, including members of the Norwegian trinity, particularly Saga, which hoped to develop its first big field, Snorre. The prospects of a queue also created conflict between local administrations (municipalities and counties) anticipating onshore investment and new jobs. It also created tension between the MPE and a more aggressive NPD (which had angered some offshore consortia and their allies by attempting to influence offshore construction plans). Each of these groups had their political supporters in the Storting, where the final struggle took place in early 1988. Eventually the Ministry struck a compromise that satisfied most parties by pledging to raise its yearly investment target (from NOK 25 to NOK 27 billion) and by reducing the government stake in Snorre (to protect taxpayers). The experience, however, demonstrated the political Pandora's box that opened when the state managed the pace of offshore investment.

A less messy experience of state intervention in field depletion occurred in the early 1990s when the Norwegian state used its authority granted by the *Petroleum Activities Act 1985* to ensure that 'as much as possible of the petroleum in place ... will be produced' (s 20 §1) (the so-called 'prudent production requirements') to increase the life of its oldest field, Ekofisk. When oil was initially discovered in 1969, the field's lifetime was estimated to be 25 years (Kongsnes, 2004). The original 1971 plan for Development and Operations (PDO) estimated the total recovery of petroleum from the field to be only 17 percent due to the presence of complex chalk formations (NPD, 2023e). Predictions for recovery from the field in 1988 improved to 20–30 percent. In the early 1990s, however, field subsidence and poor maintenance raised safety concerns prompting Phillips to seek permission to decommission parts of the Ekofisk complex. The NPD rejected the request and directed Phillips to submit a revised PDO for the field. The resulting redevelopment of Ekofisk production facilities and the use of increased recovery techniques (especially water injection in the limestone field) means that the total recovery for the field will now be closer to 50 percent when the field is decommissioned in 2050 or later (Norwegian Petroleum, 2023a).

International Pressure

Depletion policy captured the attention of domestic interests in both countries, but geopolitics and instability in oil markets also opened Britain and Norway to international pressures. For instance, increasing Cold War tensions in the early 1980s brought North Sea gas production to the attention of the new Reagan Administration in the US. A planned pipeline from Siberia to western Europe, circumventing Soviet satellite states and independent of the old Soviet export pipeline system through eastern Europe, angered US officials who argued that gas sales would boost the Soviet economy and foster energy dependence on Russia. The solution, in their view, was increased exports from Norway, which was just beginning to develop its gas resources. US officials, perhaps influenced by knowledge of Norway's official depletion policy, seemed to think Norway was purposely delaying the development of its massive reserves. From Norway's perspective, the Reagan Administration did not appreciate the cost and technical difficulty of developing offshore gas fields in the far north.[3] Norwegian gas would eventually flow to Europe, but not soon.

The Soviet pipeline controversy also affected the UK. The US did not expect Britain to supply the continent with natural gas, but it did push the country to end any British involvement in the construction of the pipeline. In December 1981, in response to the declaration of martial law in Poland, the Reagan administration prohibited the shipment of any energy equipment with US content to the Soviet Union. It then extended the embargo to equipment produced by overseas subsidiaries of US companies and equipment manufactured under license from American firms. Europe, including the UK, defied the American embargo and shipped pipeline materials to the Soviets. European defiance forced the US to end its embargo in late 1982. In the end, neither Norway nor Britain altered its policies in response to US pressure.

Pressure from the US in the 1980s proved easier to deflect than demands from OPEC. The stunning jump in oil prices in the late 1970s caused primarily by the Iranian Revolution forced consuming countries to conserve power, seek alternative forms of energy, and encourage petroleum production in high-cost provinces outside OPEC control. By late 1980, the first signs of an oil glut – no doubt intensified by North Sea oil production – began to affect OPEC cohesion. Saudi Arabia defended the official price by trimming its own production, but 'spot prices' on the open market continued to fall. Unable to sell their oil, BNOC and Statoil cut their official contract prices in early 1983 causing an angry response from OPEC. BNOC may have reached a tacit agreement with Saudi Arabia to help maintain official prices, which agitated the US enough that it accused BNOC of being 'the 14th OPEC member' (*Financial Times,* 1985, p. 8). Spot prices, however, continued to undermine official prices, and in October 1984 Statoil reduced its rates and BNOC followed. OPEC stepped up its attacks on Norway and Britain, accusing them of destabilizing the market, even as its own members persisted in cheating on their quotas. By late 1985, Saudi Arabia's frustration boiled over. In December, with oil selling for $28/bbl, it opened its oil spickets and flooded the market. By August 1986, Saudi Light was selling for $7/bbl, and North Sea Brent for $9/bbl (see Figure 3.1).

---

[3]   Particularly the formation of condensates from heavy hydrocarbon fractions, which pose enormous risks.

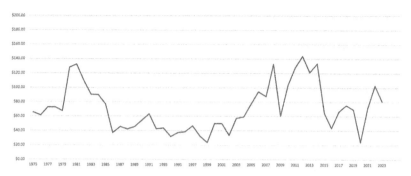

Note: *Data points taken from February of each year.
Source: Brent crude oil. (2023). Trading Economics. Retrieved from https://tradingeconomics.
com/commodity/brent-crude-oil.

Figure 3.1   Brent crude oil price in USD/bbl, 1975–2023

The Saudis clearly tried to drive North Sea producers to their knees. They failed, however, to close any wells. OPEC attempts to force Britain to adopt production restraints had little impact; Britain had no reason to alienate its allies and, moreover, stood to gain more than it would lose from low oil prices. But Norway was more vulnerable. Unlike the UK, Norway had not yet reached its oil production peak and planned to increase production by 25 percent by the end of the decade. Continued low oil prices would certainly hurt. In addition, domestic political interests criticized the Willoch government for abandoning Norway's role as a bridgebuilder to the developing world by refusing to cooperate with OPEC. Norwegians, especially those on the left, were pained by attacks from the 'Third World' on their moral integrity. Thus, when Labour's Gro Harlem Brundtland replaced Willoch as Prime Minister in spring 1986, some accommodation with OPEC was expected. Indeed, in May 1986, Brundtland announced that Norway would 'contribute towards' global price stabilization if OPEC countries could reach an agreement among themselves (Udgaard, 1987, p. 28). OPEC took several months to reach an agreement, but soon after it announced production cuts, Norway declared its intention to take 10 percent of its November and December production off the market by redirecting it to its strategic oil reserve. In January, it announced it would regulate production to a level 7.5 percent lower than it would have been without controls. Norwegian output would continue to rise, just at a slightly lower rate. OPEC appreciated the support, although the US, Britain, and most of the oil companies (not including Norsk Hydro and Statoil) opposed it. At home, the opposition criticized Labour for limiting Norway's freedom to set its own depletion policy. When a new non-socialist government took power in 1990, Conservative Party Prime Minister Jan Peder Syse ended Norway's production restraints in response to OPEC's failure to reign in the production of its own members.

Both domestic and international forces pressured Britain and Norway to limit the rate of petroleum production on their continental shelves. Both governments had the authority to regulate depletion, but only the Norwegian state effectively limited production (see Figures 3.2 and 3.3).

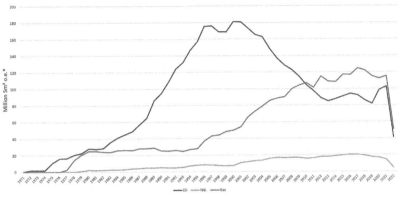

Note: *Million Sm³ o.e., natural gas is not normalized to 40 MJ/Sm³.
Source: Norwegian Petroleum. (2022). Production forecasts. Retrieved from https://
www.norskpetroleum.no/en/production-and-exports/production-forecasts/#:~:text=In%20
2022%2C%20Norway%20produced%20232,somewhat%20lower%20than%20in%202021.

Figure 3.2   Norwegian oil and gas production, 1971–2022

TAXATION

Britain

Rising oil prices in the late 1970s gave states the upper hand over the petroleum companies in their efforts to increase oil tax revenue. Britain instituted its new offshore tax system in 1975, which featured a special Petroleum Revenue Tax (PRT). By early 1978, state officials in several departments learned just how much the companies were profiting from their offshore activities and how government revenues were falling far short of expectations. The Labour government, therefore, proposed raising the PRT rate from 45 to 60 percent, decreasing the 'uplift' from 75 to 35 percent, and reducing the tax-free oil allowance from one million to half a million tons, with a total accumulation of five million (down from ten million) tons allowed. The Treasury estimated that the government take of offshore profits would rise from 70 to 75 percent.

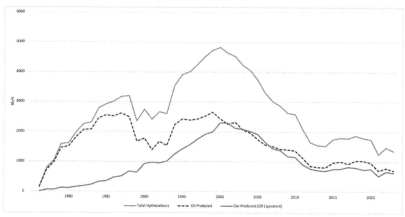

Source: North Sea Transition Authority (NSTA). (2024). UKCS production. Retrieved https://www.nstauthority.co.uk/data-centre/nsta-open-data/production/.

Figure 3.3   *British oil and gas production, 1976–2023*

Labour suffered defeat in the 1979 election before passing the new tax rates, but the Conservatives supported the changes and included them in the July 1979 *Finance Act* as oil prices continued to rise. The Thatcher government raised the PRT to 70 percent in March 1980, lifting the total government take to 83 percent, which angered the companies who thought the government was balancing the budget on their backs. But the pressure continued. In November 1980, the government announced the creation of a fourth-tier tax (added to royalties, corporate tax, and the PRT) called the Supplementary Petroleum Duty (SPD), set at 20 percent of a field's gross revenues. The SPD and other measures ensured a significant and immediate revenue flow from the offshore sector to government coffers. The companies, however, recognized the new, very complex system as a threat to marginal fields and began cancelling some of the smaller projects under development. The government responded to company pressure by abolishing the SPD and replacing it with an Advanced Petroleum Revenue Tax (APRT) that did not add to a company's tax bill but moved forward payment of a portion of the PRT. The changes failed to satisfy the companies, so the government launched a revision of the offshore tax regime in 1983 (see Table 3.2).

The government announced the 1983 reforms in its March budget, to the jubilation of the companies. The simplified tax system divided North Sea fields outside the southern gas basin into old fields (approved for develop-ment before 1 April 1982) and new fields. Old fields remained under the pre-1983 system, although minus the APRT, which was to be phased out by

Table 3.2   *The evolving British petroleum tax regime, 1979–88*

Year	Major Changes
1979	• PRT raised to 60 percent
	• Uplift lowered to 35 percent
	• Oil allowance lowered to 500,000 tons/year; total accumulation limited to 5 million tons
1980	• PRT raised to 70 percent
1981	• Introduction of Supplementary Petroleum Duty
	• SPD set at 20 percent
	• Limitation of uplift and safeguard provision
1982	• PRT raised to 75 percent
	• SPD abolished after 1982
	• Introduction of Advanced Petroleum Revenue Tax (APRT)
	• APRT set at 20 percent
1983	• APRT phased out by the end of 1986
	• Exploration costs deducted from PRT
	• Royalty abolished for 'new' fields (approved after 1 April 1982)
	• Oil allowance raised back to 1 million tons/year for 10 years for 'new' fields
1987	• R&D costs deducted from PRT
	• 10 percent of capital costs on 'new' fields (approved after 17 March 1987) deducted from total PRT payment
1988	• Royalties eliminated on 'new' fields (approved after 31 March 1982) in the Southern Basin
	• Oil allowance for old fields in the Southern Basin cut to 200,000 tons/year

Source: Nelsen (1991, p. 141). Used by permission.

the end of 1986. New fields would operate under a new system designed to encourage exploration by eliminating the regressive royalty payments and allowing deductions from the PRT. The oil companies welcomed the changes and the period of tax stability they ushered in. They responded by increasing exploration on the UKCS and bringing forward several projects ready for development. Meanwhile, the Treasury watched offshore tax proceeds soar to 8 percent of total government revenue (see Figure 3.4).

Norway

In Norway, officials waited until late 1979 before acknowledging an on-going review of offshore tax policy. After a period of consultation with the private petroleum companies – which were wholly aware of their weak bargaining position – the government announced a set of changes to the tax system that became law in mid-1980. The new system included an increase in the Special Petroleum Tax (set in 1975) from 25 to 35 percent, a reduction in uplift from 150 to 100 percent over 15 years, and a reduction in the time allowed to

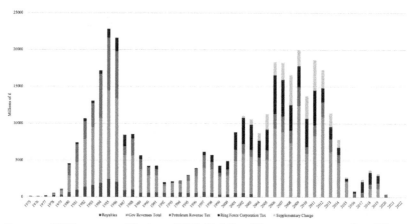

Source: HM Revenues and Customs. (2020). Statistics of Government revenues from UK Oil and Gas production. Retrieved from https://assets.publishing.service.gov.uk/government/uploads/system/uploads/attachment_data/file/902798/Statistics_of_government_revenues_from_UK_oil_and_gas_production__July_2020_for_publication.pdf.

Figure 3.4   *British tax on offshore oil production*

Table 3.3   *The evolving Norwegian petroleum tax regime, 1980–86*

Year	Major Changes
1980	• Special Petroleum Tax raised to 35 percent
	• Uplift reduced to 100 percent over 15 years
	• Tax credit period reduced to 6 months
1986	• Special Petroleum Tax reduced to 30 percent
	• Royalty lowered to 0 for 'new' fields (approved after 1 January 1987)
	• Capital costs deducted from Special Tax upon expenditure
	• Uplift eliminated for investments made after 1 January 1987
	• Production allowance of 15 percent of field's gross income introduced for 'new' fields

Source: Nelsen (1991, p. 141). Used by permission.

companies to delay paying their taxes (the 'tax credit period') from one year to six months (see Table 3.3). These changes raised the projected government take to 82 percent. The companies were not happy, but they had little leverage in a booming market. Their complaints went unheeded – even as the market began to weaken, the British loosened their system, and marginal fields went undeveloped. Unlike the British government, the Norwegians – who were less anxious to rush development – refused to respond to calls for offshore relief.

All of this changed when the bottom fell out of the oil market in 1986. In Norway, the crash raised howls from the petroleum companies, now represented more forcefully by their previously low-profile trade association the Norwegian Industry Association for Oil Companies (NIFO). Norwegian industry and the shipowners also advocated for offshore tax relief as business began to dry up. The government launched a study of the issue that soon saw the Ministry of Finance and MPE squabbling over which offshore developments deserved tax concessions. The Ministry of Finance sought to minimize the impact to revenues by raising taxes on profitable fields while cutting them on new fields. The MPE argued for lowering the tax bill for all NCS developments. When the government failed to act, companies began threatening to boycott the Eleventh Round of licensing. Worse, four out of the five members of the Troll consortium moved to declare the Troll field uneconomical under the current tax regime. The threats focused minds and the new Brundtland government forged a compromise that protected revenues while offering incentives to develop new fields. The government did not eliminate the Special Petroleum Tax but reduced it to 30 percent and allowed capital costs to be deducted upon expenditure. An additional deduction in the form of a production allowance of 15 percent of a field's gross income was introduced for new fields approved after 1 January 1987. In addition, royalties were eliminated entirely for these new fields. The new tax rules (passed by the Storting in December 1986) eliminated the threat of company flight from the Norwegian sector, but government offshore revenues dropped 60 percent from 1985 to 1987, recovering only slightly by the end of the decade (see Figure 3.5).

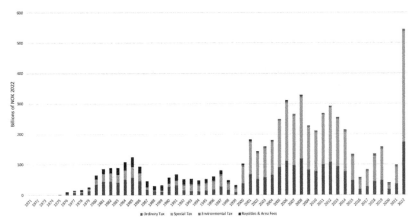

Source: Norwegian Petroleum. (2023b). The government's revenues. Retrieved from https://www.norskpetroleum.no/en/economy/governments-revenues/#:~:text=The%20total%20payment%20form%20tax,NOK%2077%20billion%20in%202023.

Figure 3.5   *Norwegian tax on offshore production*

The British tax system, having already undergone reform in 1983, was better able to handle the crash of 1986. The regime proved flexible enough that fields profitable before the crash remained profitable after. The companies sought and received some adjustments: research and development costs could be deducted from PRT, the ring fence around individual fields was loosened, and royalties were eliminated on new gas fields in the southern basin (but partially offset by a cut in the oil allowance for old fields). But these were all relatively minor adjustments that benefitted some offshore developments more than others. The British government in the late 1980s effectively divided the companies and prevented them from calling with one voice for deeper tax cuts.

PARTICIPATION

British and Norwegian offshore policies diverged in large and small ways in the 1980s, but outside observers would have been forgiven for not noticing a major deviation from the standard North Sea system established in the 1970s if they were looking only at licensing, offshore taxation, and (stepping back a ways) depletion policy. Add to the mix, however, state participation and the divergence suddenly looks dramatic and substantial. In the 1980s, the Tories reversed Labour's signature decision to follow Norway and increase offshore state control by creating a government-owned oil company. This privatization of the UKCS transformed the British state's offshore regime to that of regulatory intervention.

Britain

During the 1979 General Election campaign, the British Conservatives attacked BNOC, but offered little indication of what they would do with the company once in office (Forster and Zillman, 1983). All knew, however, that BNOC's special privileges during licensing rounds would end. Thus, in July 1979, the Thatcher government's DoE removed BNOC's 51 percent interest in each new license, its right to sit on all operating committees, its preferential treatment when awarded licenses, its ability to receive licenses outside of official rounds, its right of first-refusal on all ownership interests that come available, its exemption from PRT, and its role as advisor to the Ministry. In short, BNOC lost all forms of state support and became just another offshore oil company.

But the Thatcher government was not satisfied with stripping BNOC's privileges. The Treasury was particularly keen on selling BNOC assets to relieve budget pressures (Vickers and Wright, 1989). The company, however, successfully fended off these attempts by proving itself valuable during the aftermath of the Iranian Revolution, which threatened oil supplies. Once again, the company raised funds for the Treasury through the forward sale of oil.

But the reprieve was only temporary. The government had not yet developed a comprehensive privatization plan for national corporations, but Secretary of State for Energy David Howell was busy sowing the seeds of such a plan.

Secretary Howell attempted to privatize the exploration and development activities of BNOC in early 1981, but had to abandon the effort after failing to secure the full backing of the cabinet. In the summer of 1981, however, Chancellor of the Exchequer Sir Geoffrey Howe indicated that the government was considering the sale to the private sector of key government-owned corporations, including BNOC and British Gas. The Conservatives were now ready to pursue a comprehensive privatization policy that placed every public-sector company under scrutiny. The policy environment had completely shifted: 'state companies now had to justify their position in the public sector, rather than the government having to justify its plans to sell them off' (Nelsen, 1991, p. 159).

Leading the Thatcher government's new privatization plan was an enthusiastic monetarist named Nigel Lawson, who took over from David Howell as Secretary of State for Energy. Thatcher would later name Lawson Chancellor of the Exchequer. Lawson did not significantly alter Howell's plan to privatize public offshore companies, but he provided the necessary leadership to gain cabinet approval in late 1981. The announced plan, like the previous Howell plan, called for BNOC to be divided into two parts: offshore operations would be spun off into a private company called Britoil, while BNOC would remain as an oil trading company. In addition, British Gas was to sell its offshore oil production assets and end its monopsony position as Britain's only offshore gas buyer. Labour opposed the plan as the first step in what party leaders suspected was a full-scale sell-off of all nationalized industries. To avoid a showdown over specific parts of the plan, the Conservative government put forward an enabling Bill that granted the Secretary of State the authority to carry out the privatization plan but avoided putting any of the details in the legislation. The *Oil and Gas (Enterprise) Act* received royal assent in June 1982 and offshore privatization commenced.

Privatization turned out to be more difficult than expected. BNOC first created Britoil as a subsidiary to hold all its offshore activities. In August 1982, the company then transferred Britoil's shares to the Secretary of State for Energy. At that point, the process ran into difficulty. DoE wished to sell Britoil, but needed to balance three objectives: placing the majority of shares in private hands, spreading those shares as widely as possible, and maximizing revenue for the Treasury. A weak oil market and declining oil company share prices raised fears that the government would be selling Britoil at exactly the wrong time. Lawson, however, was not persuaded. Furthermore, efforts to maximize revenues from a sale of Britoil shares by proposing an auction led many to point out that small investors – the ones the Thatcher government wanted buying shares – found auctions intimidating. In response, the DoE made special arrangements for small investors in order to limit their risk. Creative concessions, however, made little difference in the end. In November 1982, the DoE offered the public 51 percent of the shares of Britoil, but the offering flopped. Only 26 percent of the shares were sold (9 percent to small investors), leaving the underwriters with 185 million shares that were soon selling for 20 percent below their initial price. The Treasury pulled in £637 million, but the event soured the financial community on government offerings.

Next on the block were BGC's oil assets. The DoE, now under Lawson's successor Peter Walker, followed the Britoil script and consolidated the assets into a new oil company (Enterprise Oil), transferred the shares to the Secretary of State, and announced that the shares would be sold to the public in June 1984. Conditions seemed right for a successful offering. The financial community deemed Enterprise a more promising company than Britoil, and the Ministry set a more conservative initial offering price. The press expected a better result. It did not materialize. Oil prices slid on news of violence in the Persian Gulf and investors closed their purses. In fact, 49 percent of the shares were bid for by a single mining company, RTZ, prompting Walker to veto the bid as a threat to the independence of the fledgling company. This action left 73 percent of the (declining) shares in the hands of the underwriters. Another failure. Undeterred, the Thatcher government decided to offer the remaining 49 percent of Britoil shares (while maintaining ownership of a 'golden share' that allowed the government to block unwanted takeovers) even as the oil market weakened further. This time the DoE deliberately undervalued the shares by 10 percent, which caused the offering to be oversubscribed and share prices to rise 22 percent. The government reaped £449 million in 1985, just before the oil price collapse. The Thatcher government finally had a win.

Britoil and BNOC did not survive the 1980s (although Enterprise Oil lasted until 2002). Britoil was vulnerable from the start. BP made a strong bid for the new company in late 1987 but Britoil resisted. Eventually BP raised its stake to 54 percent of the shares, forcing the government to decide if it would exercise its right as holder of the 'golden share' to block the takeover. Labour and the Scottish lobby strongly objected to BP's bid, but after a series of talks between BP, Britoil, and the government, Lawson decided to let BP purchase the company, but only after having agreed to certain conditions. According to the arrangement, Britoil was to become a subsidiary of BP, headquartered in Scotland, with responsibility for all upstream petroleum activities on the British, Norwegian, and Irish continental shelves. In addition, BP was to increase its investment in the North Sea and to allow the government, through continued use of its 'golden share', to control some leadership appointments at Britoil. Thus, in 1988 Britoil ceased to be an independent company, but the government had made sure it protected its Scottish interests and deflected criticism from the offshore goods and supplies industry.

BNOC, now shorn of its offshore activities, remained a price setter in the international oil trading market with approximately 870,000 barrels of crude oil passing through daily. The company took control of the oil that offshore companies were required to turn over to the government. The oil came in the form of royalty payments (260,000 b/d), or as part of participation agreements (435,000 b/d) that required BNOC to purchase oil at a fixed-term price (and did not require the companies to buy the oil back at the same price as required by 'normal' participation agreements). The remaining oil (175,000 b/d) came from small companies that produced limited amounts they preferred to sell to BNOC rather than risk major trading losses in the open market. The problem BNOC faced was that it was consigned a great deal of oil with no place to store it. In a tight market, oil would sell as fast as it came in. But in a weak market BNOC had no way to withhold oil from the trading floor to await better prices. Rather, it was forced to dump its oil on the spot market (the global free market) at prices below the term price it was paying producers. And, since BNOC was a major trader, the more oil it dumped on the market, the more the price fell. It became a vicious cycle.

The government would likely have dissolved BNOC soon after its creation had it not found the trading company a convenient policy tool. According to a House Energy Committee investigation, the Thatcher government pressed BNOC to maintain a high-term price (which remained a benchmark for many other market suppliers) to sustain tax revenues from the oil sector. Furthermore, the Committee maintained that the government used BNOC's term price to covertly support OPEC's pricing structure (Parliamentary Energy Committee, 8 March 1985, pp. x, xiii). The government's efforts, of course, could only be effective in the short term. Market forces eventually won out forcing BNOC to cut its term price in February 1983 and October 1984. By the end of 1984, BNOC was out of money and had to appeal to Parliament to help it pay for trading losses. The company was now more of a liability than an asset. The government decided to dissolve BNOC to the joy of the offshore companies, but over the loud objections of the Labour opposition. BNOC's responsibilities for trading royalty oil were transferred to a new agency called the Oil and Pipelines Agency (OPA), as were its participation rights. The state continued to negotiate participation agreements with each offshore consortium, but not for ownership of offshore licenses (all of which had been transferred to Britoil) – only for the right (under the care of the OPA) to access oil in a state of emergency. The government then waived its right to take ownership of participation oil under normal circumstances, so it no longer needed an oil trading company to handle its share of offshore oil production. BNOC was thus dissolved in March 1986.

By early 1986, the British state was no longer involved in offshore petroleum activities, but it still owned Britain's dominant gas buyer and distributer, the British Gas Corporation. BGC, however, was next on the block. The government decided to sell British Gas as a whole, which managed to elicit opposition from both the left and right of the political spectrum. The left believed customers were best served by a state-owned company that put consumers first. The right believed customers were best served by companies operating in a competitive market. Neither would get its way: the left would see BGC sold; the right would see a private monopoly replace a public monopoly. To address some of the right's concerns, the government created an American-style regulatory agency called the Office of Gas Supply (OFGAS) to oversee what amounted to a public utility in private hands. In December 1986, the government sold four billion shares of BGC to the public for £5.5 billion, by far the best result from the sale of a state petroleum company. The sale, however, meant that the British state was now out of the petroleum business.

Norway

The Norwegian state was not – nor did it plan to be – out of the petroleum business. As in Britain, a tension emerged in Norway over the state-owned petroleum company, Statoil. By the early 1980s its gross profit was close to Norway's GDP, and many were questioning its willingness to flex its political muscles to gain special advantages in the licensing system, including access to the best acreage (Thurber and Istad, 2010, p. 8). Could a state company be both profitable and a policy tool? Could it serve both the market and the state? The Thatcher government answered 'no', but the Norwegian center-right governments chose to remain fully invested on the NCS while adjusting the balance between government control and Statoil independence.

The Willoch government came to power after promising not to sell Statoil, but to limit its power. The policy of 'wing-clipping', as it came to be known, offered to give Statoil greater freedom to pursue its commercial interests in exchange for fewer privileges and more financial discipline. Surprisingly, the government found some support among civil servants in the MPE 'who had felt themselves to be ridden over roughshod' by a state-owned company that sometimes used its political connections to bypass the Ministry (Krogh, 2023). Left-wing parties led by Labour, however, accused the government of preparing to privatize Statoil, a charge the government flatly denied (Nelsen, 1991, p. 170). The state had the upper hand, but the issue threatened to undermine Statoil's commercial activities. Thus, the government entered talks with the opposition to settle Statoil's status and prevent major policy changes after changes of government. The discussions resulted in a compromise reached in late 1984 and implemented in 1985 (Austvik, 2009). Under the new arrangements, the state continued to control at least 50 percent of each existing and future license, but its share was divided into two parts: Statoil took approximately 20 percent (for existing licenses the share was decided on a field-by-field basis), while the larger share was assigned to a new entity called the State's Direct Financial Interest (SDFI), which was managed by Statoil. The SDFI paid its share of development costs directly through the state budget, with its share of field revenue going straight into the Treasury. Statoil maintained its full voting rights in the consortia, but voting was no longer weighted.

The Willoch government's wing-clipping of Statoil did not extend to the gas market. In 1986, the MPE created a Gas Negotiation Committee (GFU) to negotiate all gas sales from the NCS. Only Norwegian companies could join government officials on the committee (to prevent foreign petroleum companies from sitting on both sides of the table), which gave Norsk Hydro, Saga, and particularly Statoil considerably more weight in dealing with a consortium of gas buyers that together formed a monopsony for European natural gas (Austvik, 2009).

The Norwegians modified the distribution of authority and revenues on the NCS in the mid-1980s, but they did not lessen state control. The new arrangements put more of the state's offshore revenue under Storting control, but allowed Statoil greater freedom to raise private capital and invest downstream or overseas. Statoil remained a state-owned company with governmental responsibilities (primarily as a tool of depletion policy and Norwegianization), but was now freer to make commercially sound decisions. The tension between commercial and governmental responsibilities remained for Statoil, but the balance had shifted slightly toward the commercial side. Any slack in state control left behind by Statoil's new commercial freedom was taken up by the MPE: the state owned a large stake in virtually every commercial activity on the NCS. Statoil was no longer in control, but the state was (Austvik, 2009, p. 115).

The compromise of 1984 spurred Statoil's development at home and abroad. During the 1980s, the company exercised its right to assume operatorship of important fields. Its first targets were Statfjord and Heidrun, both keys to future activities on the NCS. The Conservative party opposed the transfers of control from Mobil (Statfjord) and Conoco (Heidrun) to the state company, as did the NPD, but Labour and the Conservative's two coalition partners (the Center and Christian People's parties) pressed for the change and won the day. Statoil took over Statfjord in January 1987 and Heidrun in October 1995. In June 1996, it became operator of Troll. Thus, by the mid-1990s – after also acquiring a stake in Ekofisk in 1988 – Statoil operated or had a stake in every major field on the NCS – a remarkable achievement. During this period, the company also began operations beyond Norwegian waters. Its first foray was into the Dutch sector in 1983 where it joined a consortium that found two minor oil fields. Soon the company was operating in Danish waters, and by 1987 it was exploring on the continental shelves of Britain, West Germany, and Sweden. Beyond Europe, Statoil began operating in China, Malaysia, and Thailand.

While Statoil expanded its geographical reach, it also started the process of integrating its operations by investing in downstream activities, including pet-rochemicals, gasoline distribution, and sales. By the late 1980s, the company was an integrated multinational oil company with significant petrochemical and refining capacity and a Europe-wide gasoline brand called Norol. But trouble was on the horizon. Statoil, through a joint-owned subsidiary called Rafinor, had invested in a small refinery at Mongstad on Norway's west coast that it wanted to expand. The issue split Norwegian politics along a center-periphery rather than a left-right divide. The commercial center, represented by the Conservative party and the major ministries, believed that more than doubling Mongstad's capacity in a weak market was not commercially viable, while the districts and their associated parties argued that it would create good-paying jobs. Statoil raised eyebrows by engaging in a massive lobbying campaign in the Storting and eventually won approval of its Mongstad plans in June 1984. The project ran almost immediately into financial problems, which the company leadership kept hidden from the government until mid-1987, when Statoil informed the MPE that cost overruns amounted to NOK 3.8 billion and rising. Overnight the scandal called into question Statoil's motives and the government's ability to control the company's decisions. Thus, a crucial question emerged: would the state control Statoil, or Statoil the state? As the 1980s closed, Statoil was reorganized into three divisions (exploration and produc-tion, refining and marketing, and petrochemicals) like other multinational oil companies. But political disagreement over what else – if anything – should be done to reign in the company put off further reform into the 1990s.

DIVERGENCE

The 1980s saw the divergence of offshore policy in Britain and Norway, but only in two crucial areas: depletion and participation. Regulation and taxation remained very similar. The UK experimented a bit more with auctioning blocks but returned to a fully discretionary system. Norway tried to maintain its high-tax regime on the continental shelf but eventually gave in to market forces and reformed the tax system to look much like Britain's. Both countries, of course, continued to use their licensing systems to support their domestic offshore goods and supplies industries.

Britain and Norway, however, diverged modestly over depletion policy. Both Britain and Norway had the legal right to regulate petroleum production, but found it difficult to exercise its authority in a high-cost, high-risk province where companies remained vulnerable to domestic policy shifts and external shocks. British officials tinkered briefly with development delays to benefit the state budget, but abandoned such efforts quickly and returned to a policy of encouraging rapid offshore development. The Norwegians feared a flood of petrodollars, but realized that limiting production would be counterproductive. Instead, officials decided to regulate the flow of offshore investment, which promised to keep money flowing to the coastal districts. More important, however, was Norway's willingness to cooperate with OPEC. Britain may have briefly and tacitly supported official OPEC crude prices, but Norway explicitly limited production in coordination with major producing countries. It would be difficult to imagine Britain ever following suit.

The most visible divergence, of course, concerned state participation. The British state – under the political control of the Tories – sold its petroleum enterprises and let go dormant its participation rights in offshore licenses, while the Norwegians expanded the reach of Statoil to every part of the NCS, and then beyond the borders of Norway. The Norwegian government found it necessary to exert greater control of its state-owned company, but there was little chance the authorities would attempt to privatize Statoil fully. The Norwegian system would remain participatory, while the British offshore regime moved to a regulatory regime.

How do we explain this divergence of policy? The system conditions remained very similar for both countries (see Figures 3.6 and 3.7). The volatile price of oil during the 1980s altered – in similarly volatile ways – the dynamics between the companies and the states. When prices were high at the beginning of the 1980s, the states very much had the upper hand and used their taxing power to extract a larger proportion of revenue from company profits. When prices declined later in the decade, the companies regained some of their clout and forced tax reforms in both countries that encouraged offshore exploration and continued production from small fields.

Pressure groups in both countries continued to press the states to intervene on their behalf. But the pressure on the Norwegian government proved more intense and politically effective than that in Britain. In Britain the oil companies carried clout, as did the various interests pressing for petroleum-related jobs. These groups sometimes succeeded in convincing officials to cede to their wishes, as happened in the Sun Oil saga. Norwegian groups, however – primarily those representing interests in the coastal districts, but also big business, the environment, and even Statoil – proved weightier in this period because they could appeal directly to the Storting, which had to approve major projects. As we saw, this pressure altered important policy decisions, including the rate of offshore investment, the queue, and Mongstad expansion. In addition, OPEC proved more influential in Norway than in Britain. Britain remained solidly in the western consumers' camp as a member of the IEA.

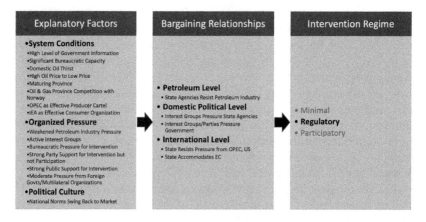

Figure 3.6   Divergence: Great Britain

Figure 3.7   Divergence: Norway

But Norway stayed aloof from the IEA and thus looked vulnerable to OPEC pressure.

Explaining the divergence in participation policy cannot rely on group pressure alone. Norwegian bureaucratic and political culture remained comfortable with a state petroleum company as a tool of government policy. Some elements of the political right preferred to support private or semi-private Norwegian companies. But few called for a complete privatization of the NCS; a consensus across Norway supported state participation offshore, despite the British example. Participation in the UK, however, was entirely politicized. Labour fully supported state participation: had the party remained in government through the 1980s, BNOC would have remained a state-owned company. But the Tories won the 1979 election. They did not commit to full privatization until months after they assumed office, but once they took the decision, they sold off state holdings with ideological passion. The Conservatives were content to regulate the North Sea and reap its benefits; running an integrated petroleum company was best left to the private sector. Thus, in Britain, unlike Norway, elections in this period mattered to the course of offshore policy.

In the 1980s, bargaining occurred at all three levels of interaction – petroleum, domestic political, and international – in both Britain and Norway. The oil companies remained influential, but the states held the upper hand. At the domestic political level, the interest groups were at least as strong as the oil companies in matters concerning industrial development, job creation, environmental protection, and human safety. And they were often able to move governments to decide in their favor. But at this level, the most important relationship was that of the political parties to the government. In Norway, where politics is more consensual, opposition parties and coalition partners often influenced offshore policy, in particular which Norwegian companies (state-owned or private) to favor in licensing rounds and development queues. In Britain, where politics remained adversarial, the party in government could alter policy dramatically. If the will existed, a party could completely reverse a previous government's initiative – including the dismantling of a state-owned company. Finally, the international level emerged as important in the 1980s. Production from the North Sea now impacted the global oil market, which brought international scrutiny to British and Norwegian policies. As we saw above, Britain largely ignored global pressure on its policies (from both OPEC and the US), but Norway found itself under significant pressure it could not ignore from other petroleum producing countries. Norway responded to the pressure, but did not alter its basic offshore policy regime.

4.   Reconvergence: maximizing resource recovery

In the 1970s and 1980s, the United Kingdom (UK) and Norway shifted their views on the role of the state in the North Sea. Policy initially converged on the need for state control, even participation, in the exploitation of offshore petroleum. But in the 1980s the strategy in the two countries increasingly diverged. By the mid 1990s, the UK and Norway represented opposite ends of the state-control spectrum: Norway at one end with its high level of regulation and participation (Bunter, 2002, pp. 19–20), the UK at the other with its lighter touch to regulation, and market approach to resource development. This divergence in policy, however, was short lived. In 1994, the European Union (EU) implemented its Hydrocarbon Directive (European Parliament and Council, Directive 94/22/EC, 1994), which altered the way both Norway (as a member of the newly formed European Economic Area, EEA) and Britain, as an EU Member State, allocated petroleum licenses. In addition, by the early 2000s, the rapid decline in North Sea petroleum production on the United Kingdom Continental Shelf (UKCS) forced the British to reconsider their relaxed approach to offshore activity and reintroduce a degree of state intervention, while the Norwegians moved to reduce state involvement offshore. Thus, policy began to reconverge around a more regulatory approach to offshore petroleum activity.

INTERNATIONAL CONTEXT

The three decades following the divergence of offshore policy in the 1980s saw dramatic changes that roiled the global petroleum system. The fall of the Berlin Wall, the end of the Cold War, the breakup of the Soviet Union, and the incorporation of the old Soviet sphere into the global economy in the early 1990s made Russia a petroleum superpower. Western investment poured into the Russian hydrocarbon sector and, by the turn of the century, Russian oil and gas was pouring into global markets. Energy thirsty western Europe gulped down Russian petroleum through long straws that by 2022 supplied 45 percent of Europe's natural gas, compared to the 23 percent coming from Norway (Cocklin, 2022). Even more gas from Russia was due through the soon-to-open Nord Stream 2 pipeline. As for oil, 26 percent of Europe's imports came from

Russia, via pipelines and ships, versus 9 percent from Norway (Eurostat, 2023). In short, post-Cold War Europe became deeply dependent on Russian energy, a fact only magnified by Russia's attack on Ukraine in February 2022 that turned the European energy market into a NATO-Russia battlefield. Some of the first energy casualties of the war were the Nord Stream gas pipelines (1 and 2) from Russia. Each was severed by mysterious underwater explosions in late 2022.

The end of the Cold War also brought new energy and new members to the EU. The 1993 Maastricht treaty set the stage for greater political cooperation among Member States, the adoption of a common currency and monetary policy, and the accession of eastern bloc countries eager to align with the free market democracies of the EU. The stampede of states toward the EU made some West European elites nervous. Commission President Jacques Delors had for some time worried about the impact of rapid enlargement. In response, he announced plans in 1989 to create a European Economic Space (later changed to 'Area' – EEA) as an alternative to full EU membership. The Delors plan, however, failed. The EEA agreement was signed in 1992 and implemented in 1994 (for all except Switzerland, which voted down membership in 1992), but almost all the Member States of the European Free Trade Association (EFTA), which entered the EEA, decided to apply for EU membership immediately, including Norway. The Nordic applicants and Austria negotiated accession agreements very quickly, held referenda in 1994, and joined in 1995. That is all except Norway, where the voters rejected EU membership for a second time.

Norway decided to stay out of the EU, but remain in the EEA with Switzerland, Iceland, and Lichtenstein. EEA membership allowed Norway to join the single market (with op-outs for the fishing industry), where it agreed to abide by EU rules without a seat and vote in the Council of Ministers. In the end, Norway chose not to join Britain as a member of the EU, but the two countries did become partners in the single market in the 1990s. That partnership ended, of course, with Brexit in 2020. Britain, in its shambolic exit from the EU, rejected the 'Norway option' that would have kept the country in the EEA and thus the single market. Most Brexiteers were horrified by the thought of leaving the EU, but remaining tethered to its economic regulations. Thus, technically and ironically, Britain broke free from EU regulations while Norway remained subject to them.

The price of Brent crude oil during this period remained relatively low, but stable, through the 1990s (see Figure 3.1). A dramatic rise, however, began after 2000 as the benefits of globalization and China's rapid development increased the demand for oil. The price peaked in January 2008 just under $140/bbl, but the bank crisis that took down the global financial system caused a deep recession in the developed economies collapsing demand for energy. One year later, in January 2009, Brent crude sold for $45/bbl. By January 2011 prices had climbed back up over \$100/bbl and stayed there until 2015 when the US shale oil boom added to global supplies while demand remained relatively weak. Prices recovered only to free fall in March 2020 due to the shutdown of economies across the world as a result of the COVID-19 pandemic. The reopening of economies drew the price higher, but post-pandemic inflation, rising interest rates, and war in Europe cut into any major recovery.

Significant changes took place in the gas market during this period that drastically affected the availability and price of natural gas. At the beginning of the 1990s, the old-style Groningen system remained dominant in Europe. Gas producers negotiated long-term contracts with national or regional distribution monopolies that delivered gas to customers through pipelines they owned. No open and competitive market in gas existed to set prices, so contract negotiators typically tied gas prices to crude oil or other petroleum products. Twenty years later the system had changed entirely: long-term contracts had virtually disappeared; transparent gas hubs and spot markets set prices for gas distributed the old way through pipelines and the new way via liquified natural gas (LNG) tankers; and pipeline companies (now largely separated from gas suppliers) opened their pipes to third-party distributors. Prices, now freed from petroleum benchmarks and corporate negotiations, remained relatively steady for over two decades. Dramatic spikes in price, however, started in late 2021 as tensions grew between Russia and Ukraine. The War in Ukraine began in early 2022 resulting in sanctions on Russia and pipeline explosions that severely diminished the supply of Russian gas. Overall, Russia was supplying less than 20 percent of European gas at the end of 2022 to Norway's over 20 percent (European Council, 2023). All of this was good news, of course, for Norway's gas industry.

Finally, the world after 1990 awoke to the smoldering climate crisis and took steps – small ones to be sure – to move away from carbon fuels to renewable sources of energy. The United Nations (UN) adopted in 1992 the UN Framework Convention on Climate Change (UNFCCC) that required parties to meet regularly to address climate change at gatherings of the Conference of Parties (COP), the first of which Berlin hosted in 1995. Two of these annual conferences stand out as particularly significant: COP 3 (1997) produced the Kyoto Protocol that obligated signatories to reduce greenhouse gas emissions to pre-1990 levels and the Paris Accords of COP 21 (2015), which covered climate change mitigation, adaptation, and finance. Britain and Norway have staunchly supported global efforts to combat global warming and are moving to reduce their carbon emissions by developing renewable energy sources, including on and offshore wind and hydropower. Britain has also added to its renewable mix of solar power, biofuels, and tidal power and continues to rely on nuclear power generation, which is not renewable but does not emit carbon. Both countries have also sought to develop carbon capture, usage, and storage

(CCUS) capacity, with both countries already hosting facilities recycling or sequestering carbon. Neither country can escape the fact, however, that it produces large amounts of fossil fuels that it primarily consumes (UK) or sells (Norway). Britain is less concerned that its declining offshore sector presents an image problem. But Norway, understandably, finds it more difficult to present itself to the world as a defender of the planet (and the spectacular nature that draws so many tourists to Norway!) while reaping trillions of dollars in profit from the production and sale of hydrocarbons.

The international context exerted pressure on British and Norwegian petroleum policy during the decades following the divergence of the 1980s. These pressures, combined with internal forces, pressed these governments to shift their policies in a common direction.

LICENSING

By the early 1990s, the British and Norwegian offshore petroleum provinces had reached maturity. Extensive exploration over 30 years had revealed the largest fields on both continental shelves; new discoveries of any appreciable size were becoming rare (Storting, 2011, p. 98). Production rates at existing fields were also falling due to the natural drop in pressure over time, with more and more fields reaching their point of unprofitability and decommissioning (see Figures 4.2 and 4.3). As these petroleum provinces began their decline, states and company interests diverged. Governments on the one hand wanted to squeeze the last possible drops of hydrocarbons from the ground; private companies on the other wished to halt production before starting to lose money. Policy makers managing this decline could let the companies decide when to abandon a field. But if they were intent on maximizing resource recovery while maintaining good relations with their corporate offshore partners, they had to start offering companies production incentives.

Britain and Norway had the tools for managing decline: offshore licenses and production programs. Licensing provided Britain and Norway with opportunities to encourage exploration in new, untested provinces, or in areas near or adjacent to existing fields in better-known sectors. Both governments experimented with new types of offshore licenses and new rules for conducting licensing rounds – all designed to entice companies into more exploratory drilling. Just which companies would be doing the drilling and field development had always been up to the discretion of British and Norwegian authorities who could manage activities through work programs. The awarding of licenses, however, was complicated by EU regulations affecting both countries in the 1990s. We explore these several developments in this section.

Britain

The British government responded to the maturing of its petroleum province by introducing two new licenses, Promote (2003) and Frontier (2004), to complement its Traditional license. Officials designed the Promote license to attract smaller companies with detailed knowledge of specific hydrocarbon prospects to apply for unused or unexplored territory. The Ministry waved requirements to demonstrate a minimum level of technical and environmental competence in favor of proving sufficient financial resources to conduct drilling activities. This made participation in a round attractive to companies that lacked financial and managerial capacity to mount a full-scale exploration operation. Moreover, the government set fees for the first two years of the Promote license at one-tenth the cost of its traditional counterpart (Gordon, 2011, p. 103). Of the 88 licenses awarded in the 21st Round, 54 were Promote licenses. By late 2005, 188 Promote licenses had been awarded with 35 new companies entering the UKCS ('Promote', 2005).

The Frontier licenses encouraged companies to explore in promising, but under-explored areas such as the west of Shetlands and the Rockall Basins to the northwest of Scotland. The department modified its three-term process for Frontier licenses to extend the first two terms to six years each followed by the standard 18-year third term. The first term was divided into two phases of two years, then four years. After the first phase, 75 percent of the territory was relinquished, followed by 50 percent of the remaining territory after phase two of the first term. The additional time allowed companies facing logistical and geological challenges to complete necessary assessments before having to first relinquish territory and then commit to a development plan. The Frontier licenses, which were also offered for one-tenth the fee of a Traditional license, succeeded in boosting applications and awards in the early 2000s.

The offshore licensing system went through another major revision 15 years later with the implementation of the Maximize Economic Recovery (MER) Strategy (see the next section). The Oil and Gas Authority (OGA), in accordance with the *Petroleum Act 1998*, replaced Traditional, Promote, and Frontier licenses in the 30th licensing round (2017–18) with new Innovate licenses. Expanding on the flexibility offered in the Frontier licenses, officials designed the new tools to encourage maximum recovery of petroleum from the UKCS by offering companies what amounted to customized permits.

Innovate, like the old Frontier licenses, divide the period covered by the offshore permit into three terms (NSTA, 2022):

1. Initial Term (up to nine years) – carry out the 'Exploration Work Program'.

2. Second Term (four–six years) – appraise the gathered data, submit a 'Field Development Plan', and obtain 'Development and Production Consent'.
3. Third Term (18 years, extendable) – develop the field and produce available hydrocarbons.

The Initial Term introduced the type of flexibility the companies desired. Officials divided the Initial Term into three phases that could vary in length:

1. 'Phase A is a period for carrying out geotechnical studies and geophysical data reprocessing.
2. Phase B is a period for undertaking seismic surveys and acquiring other geophysical data.
3. Phase C is for drilling.' (NSTA, 2022)

Companies applying for licenses now choose how many phases they want included in the Initial Term (Phase C is required, so one, two, or three) and how long each phase will last. Companies ready to drill, for instance, could forego the first two phases and start with Phase C. Annual fees are also placed on an escalating scale per square kilometer, thus encouraging relinquishment as soon as possible. Proving financial, technical, environmental, and safety competency can also be delayed until more is known about the area. This allows companies to put off paperwork until they decide to develop the field. The goal of these changes is to speed up exploration considerably, especially on blocks where the geology is well known. The Innovate licenses thus provide companies with the flexibility they demand to explore for smaller deposits in complicated areas or new deposits in risky areas, while maintaining regulators' ability to hold companies to written commitments.

New licensing procedures have pleased offshore companies, but British environmental groups – including Greenpeace UK, Friends of the Earth, and Uplift UK – are opposed to offshore petroleum licensing in general and advocate phasing out or halting all petroleum production on the UKCS (Halpin, 2023). These groups, for instance, lobbied hard, although unsuccessfully, against approving Rosebank, a giant field located northwest of the Shetlands (Taylor, 2023). But more radical groups that are willing to use civil disobedience to bring attention to their cause have also surfaced. Extinction Rebellion is one; Just Stop Oil is another. Just Stop Oil, for instance, has invaded Premier League football pitches, disrupted an Ashes Test match, halted Wimbledon matches, thrown soup at van Gogh's Sunflowers at the National Gallery, delayed a World Snooker Championship (by covering the table in orange powder), and blocked a Pride Parade ('Just Stop Oil', 2023). These groups have sympathetic lawmakers in Parliament, primarily in the Labour party. If Labour in the UK comes to power, environmental interests are likely to play a significant role in the new government.

Norway

The Norwegian state also experimented with a new license. Norwegian concerns were similar to those of the British, but the Norwegians focused more on known deposits in danger of being 'left behind' than on finding new fields. Officials were aware that some mature areas contained 'time-critical resources', which were known or suspected deposits (sometimes small, stranded fields that were unprofitable if developed as stand-alone projects) requiring development before nearby facilities were decommissioned. The presence of an existing production and transportation network near these smaller discoveries could reduce development costs enough to make the fields profitable. Thus, officials needed to encourage companies to explore rapidly and develop new fields before needed infrastructure disappeared (NPD, 2009, p. 33). The government also wanted to keep the offshore supply industry busy so it would not be tempted to start shrinking its Norwegian workforce.

The Ministry of Petroleum and Energy (MPE) introduced in 2003 new production licenses called Awards in Pre-Defined Areas (APA) (MPE, 2004). APA licenses were awarded in a separate set of annual rounds existing along-side the 'ordinary licensing rounds'. Typically, the MPE announces the APA round in late spring or early summer, with the application deadline scheduled for the fall. The Ministry designates predefined exploration zones that encompass all mature areas on the NCS, often adding additional areas it has declared mature (NPD, 2009, p. 33). Awards are usually made in the early months of the following year. Much like the British, the Norwegian government has encouraged small, niche companies that excel in certain types of geology to apply for APA licenses. In several instances it appointed a 'minnow' company as the operator of a technically difficult field, including, for example, the appointment in 2016 of a very small Norwegian company, Edison Norge (acquired by Sval Energi in 2021), as operator of Production License 807 (blocks 2/8, 2/9, 2/11) (NPD, 2023a).

The APA license itself is very flexible. Interested parties negotiate a work program for the area on offer that includes a bespoke set of decision points and license activities that must be met in a particular timeframe, or the license relinquished. NPD officials are open to creative approaches to resource extraction in the North Sea and want companies to experiment with new technologies. But while they encourage agility in mature areas, they are still closely overseeing the process.

The APA system seems to have worked to the satisfaction of Norwegian officials keen on managing their offshore resources efficiently. In 2008, the MPE commissioned a study of the system that concluded in 2009 (NPD, 2009). The report determined that the system was achieving its goals. Exploration activity rose in mature areas, policy was more predictable for companies making long-term plans, and a more diverse set of companies now operated offshore. Norway had successfully enticed the companies to start 'picking over the bones' of the NCS.

More problematic for Norwegian policy makers concerned with the long-term attractiveness of the NCS were the troubled traditional licensing rounds. One problem was economic. In 2016 the 23rd Round attracted 26 companies, the 25th Round (2021), only seven. As exploration moved north into harsher waters, costs (and risks) were rising making companies think twice before committing to a petroleum province of questionable economic viability. A second problem was environmental. Environmental groups had long advocated for a ban on new drilling for hydrocarbons off the Norwegian coast to slow the emission of carbon dioxide and prevent climate disaster. They also opposed the approval of new developments. The government angered the environmental groups when it gave the green light in 2023 to three North Sea developments – Breidablikk, Yggdrasil, and Tyrving – prompting Greenpeace Norway and *Natur og Ungdom* to file a lawsuit against the Norwegian state (Badgamia, 2023). The suit accuses the state of violating the Constitution and Norway's commitment to human rights, including the UN Convention on the Rights of the Child, by not protecting the environment and, therefore, the health of Norwegian citizens ('Environmentalists', 2023). The suit is not likely to succeed, but it illustrates the strong, organized opposition to the offshore industry in Norway.

The Socialist Left (SV) party represented many of these interests in the Storting and when the left bloc won the general election of 2021 and formed a center-left minority government under the leadership of Prime Minister Jonas Gahr Støre, SV secured a commitment by Labour to back a delay of the 26th Round by one year. Then in November 2022, the government announced the postponement of the round until at least 2025 as part of a budget deal with SV (Lepic, 2022). The companies complained they had not been consulted (Buli and Adomaitis, 2022). The agreement allowed the Ministry to continue offering APA licenses, but no licensing would take place in areas not considered mature.

Comparing the Systems

Britain and Norway needed to reignite company interest in their aging petroleum provinces. Licensing rounds in the 1990s failed to generate enthusiastic responses from oil and gas producers dimming the prospects for making new discoveries to replace spent fields. Both governments had to reduce participation requirements and introduce flexibility to their offshore licensing systems. In effect, they lowered the price of offshore exploration and development. The British, facing the steepest decline in production, went the farthest. The

Innovate license gave companies the flexibility to move fast when deposits were known and within reach, and more deliberately when they were charting promising but unproven territory. The Norwegians were more cautious, but still anxious to get every drop out of the mature North Sea. APA licenses gave companies permission to move fast in mature areas. They were less willing, however, to encourage companies to explore new areas, especially in the far north.

The licensing systems of Britain and Norway covering the mature areas of the continental shelves look very similar. They are designed to maximize the recovery of oil and gas. Frontier areas, however, demonstrate diverging policies. Norway has a strong environmental movement that carries political clout when the left is in power, and it does not depend on its petroleum sector to provide for its energy needs. It is too soon to tell if party politics in Norway will speed the decline of Norwegian production by the mid-century or not. Britain, with a Conservative government, has no environmental movement strong enough to halt new exploration, as Prime Minister Rishi Sunak's decision to go ahead with a large offshore round in 2023 demonstrated (Read, 2023; Wallace, 2023). Labour, however, is committed to halting the search for new sources of oil and gas.

LICENSING AND THE HYDROCARBON DIRECTIVE

Most recent changes to the licensing system were responses to the reality of maturing continental shelves. But other important changes came in response to strong outside pressure from Brussels. Britain and Norway had used discretionary licensing from the early days of offshore activity as tools of industrial policy. Both countries built significant domestic private sector exploration, development, and production capacities, and a thriving offshore services industry by favoring – sometimes explicitly, sometimes through unspoken expectations – national interests in the awarding of licenses. Naturally, the system attracted criticism from international companies that were shut out in round after round of participation in licenses covering the best prospects. They were most frustrated by the lack of transparency surrounding the criteria used to decide the winners. Petroleum companies were often unable to determine exactly what the state expected of successful applicants in terms of work programs and commitment to domestic suppliers (Sunnevåg, 2000, pp. 3–6).

In 1994, however, the EU began to pry open the 'discretion black box' with its Directive 94/22/EC, *On the Conditions for Granting and Using Authorizations* [Licenses] *for the Prospection, Exploration and Production of Hydrocarbons (1994)* – otherwise known as the 'Hydrocarbon Directive' (European Parliament and of the Council, 1994). The purpose of the Hydrocarbon Directive was three-fold. First, it sought to extend the single market to the European continental shelf by offering all 'entities possessing the necessary capabilities', regardless of nationality, an equal opportunity to obtain a petroleum license. Second, it required states to open the discretionary black box by awarding licenses 'on the basis of objective, published criteria', that, third, would be 'known in advance by all entities taking part in the procedure' (European Parliament and of the Council, 1994).

Under the Hydrocarbon Directive, EEA and EU Member States retain sovereignty over their natural resources in accordance with United Nations General Assembly Resolution 1803, ensuring they have the right to determine the areas to be made available for 'the exercise of the activities of prospecting, exploring for and producing hydrocarbons' (European Parliament and of the Council, 1994). Member States are obliged to offer all interested entities equal opportunity to apply for a license with respect to the published criteria for an award. Article 2(2), however, allows Member States to refuse any entity controlled by a foreign government or foreign nationals access to areas deemed sensitive to national security.

Article 3 details the procedure for granting licenses. States initiate the procedure by publishing a notice in the *Official Journal of the European Communities* (now *Union*) at least 90 days before the closing date for applications. Member States can also grant authorizations to petroleum activity (without initiating the procedure mentioned above) to license areas that either are available permanently, have been announced before, or have been relinquished by an entity provided the details are published in the *Official Journal* (Article 3(3)). According to Article 5, states are to grant licenses based on 'the technical and financial capability' of the applicants and the exploration and production programs they propose. In granting a license, authorities can take into consideration previous conduct, including 'any lack of efficiency and responsibility displayed by the applicants in operations under previous authorizations' (Article 5(1)). If officials consider two or more applications equal in merit based on the published criteria, 'other relevant objective and non-discriminatory criteria' may be used to make a final choice (Article 5(1)(d)). Significantly, Article 6(2) grants Member States the right to impose conditions on licensees to protect national interests, including national security, public health and safety, the environment, and taxation. Finally, Article 6(3) permits state participation in offshore activities, but prohibits discrimination against foreign providers of goods and services.

Both Britain and Norway were responsible for implementing the directive – Britain as a member of the EU until 2020, Norway as an entrant to the EEA (1 January 1994) – which they did through new petroleum legislation. The UK had already been shifting toward more objective criteria and a market-based policy of non-discrimination offshore. Britain had even experimented in the early 1970s and again in the early 1980s with open offshore auctions (see

Chapters 2–3). Thus, the passage of the UK *Petroleum Act 1998* meant relatively few changes for offshore applicants. The Act primarily consolidated
the several acts that governed offshore activity, including the *Petroleum
(Production) Act 1934*, the *Petroleum and Submarine Pipelines Act 1975*,
the *Oil and Gas (Enterprise) Act 1982*, and the *Petroleum Act 1987*. But while
Britain easily transitioned to the new European system, Norway had a more
difficult task: the very purpose of its offshore licensing system was to hide
criteria and favor domestic companies.

Norway implemented the Hydrocarbon Directive in Chapter 3 of the
Petroleum Activities Act 1996 (Norway) (PAA), Regulations 9 and 10 of
the *Petroleum Activities Regulations 1997 (Norway)* (PAR), and guidelines
issued by the NPD outlining the selection criteria for petroleum licenses
(NPD, 2022b). These acts ensured certainty and transparency in the awarding
of petroleum licenses. The new rules as outlined in the invitations to apply
for licenses opened licensing rounds to applicants registered in Norway or
the EEA, or companies registered outside the EEA who had pre-qualified as
licensees on the NCS (NPD, 2022b). Companies were invited to negotiate
a work program for a particular sector with award criteria spelled out in some
detail. Applicants would have to demonstrate that they know the geology of
their sectors, have access to adequate funding, have the capacity to exploit
any discoveries, demonstrate prior experience on the NCS or other similar
provinces, and show they have experience in risky offshore drilling. Some of
the criteria are quite specific. For instance, the invitation expresses concern
that companies know how to drill in deep water. It thus identifies a specific
qualification for some sectors:

> For production licenses in deep waters, both the appointed operator and at least one
> other participating interest shall have drilled at least one well on the Norwegian
> Continental Shelf as operator or have equivalent relevant operational experience
> outside the NCS. In the production license one participating interest shall have
> drilled in deep waters as operator. (NPD, 2022b)

Thus, Norway opened its licensing process to all qualified companies no
matter where they came from as long as they conducted activities in the 'proper
manner'. This proper manner provision included considerations for national
security, public order, public health, transport, safety, protection of biological
resources and national treasures, systematic resource management, and the
need to ensure fiscal revenues. The Norwegian state also made its decision
criteria open to public scrutiny. Thus, its licensing system looked very much
like Britain's.

The Hydrocarbon Directive and the maturing of the North Sea petroleum
province changed conditions for offshore regulation. A reconvergence of

British and Norwegian regulation of North Sea petroleum could be seen in the changes they made to their licensing systems.

DEPLETION

By the 1990s, it was clear to both Britain and Norway that peak petroleum production was nearing (see Figures 3.2 and 3.3, p. 59). In fact, both offshore provinces reached peaks at the turn of the millennium: oil and gas production in the UK in 1999 (Department for Business, Energy and Industrial Strategy, 2019); oil production in Norway in 2001 (NPD, 2018). Norwegian gas production (and perhaps total petroleum production) has likely not yet peaked but may do so – and begin a slow decline – by the mid-2020s.

In the twenty-first century, the British and Norwegian states have used rather coercive policy tools to encourage companies to maximize production on declining fields. Responsibility for production, as we have seen, falls to the company operating the field. Operators may employ a range of technical tools to enhance petroleum recovery, which include gas or water injection to increase well pressure, and chemical or biological injection to loosen oil from its host rock for more efficient removal. Enhanced recovery is costly, which may discourage consortia from prolonging the life of a field. To counter the tendency for companies to abandon fields before they are fully depleted, states hold companies to elements of the production licenses requiring consortia to maximize recovery (Muggeridge, et. al., 2014). From the beginning, the British and Norwegian states regulated extraction through the licensing system. In the late 1970s through the 1980s, however, both states participated in the production of petroleum and could use their ownership rights as an additional tool to extend field life. When the British state sold its assets on the UKCS, however, the companies operating in Britain were freer to abandon fields without investing in enhanced recovery.

Peak oil in the North Sea got the attention of officials on both shores of the petroleum province, which sparked a re-evaluation of government goals for the petroleum industry. As noted by the Norwegian MPE in 2002, 'The government must be willing to consider whether established principles and the prevailing policy framework create the right incentives for enhanced value creation, and possibly adapt policies to ensure resources are not wasted' (MPE, 2001–2002, p. 19). The desire to look hard at depletion policy was evident in both state bureaucracies, but the Norwegians were first to get serious about reform.

Norway

Norwegian policy strongly favored maximizing petroleum recovery before oil production peaked at the turn of the century. The *Petroleum Activities Act 1985* set the goal of maximum depletion and the *Petroleum Activities Act 1996* (NPD, 1996) reiterated the mandate:

> Production of petroleum shall take place in such a manner that as much as possible of the petroleum in place in each individual petroleum deposit, or in several deposits in combination, will be produced. The production shall take place in accordance with prudent technical and sound economic principles and in such a manner that waste of petroleum or reservoir energy is avoided. The licensee shall carry out continuous evaluation of production strategy and technical solutions and shall take the necessary measures in order to achieve this. (Section 4–2)

These legislative instruments gave state officials great discretion to direct petroleum activities 'for the benefit of the Norwegian society as a whole'. As the 1996 Act put it,

> the resource management shall provide revenues to the country and shall contribute to ensuring welfare, employment and an improved environment, as well as to the strengthening of Norwegian trade and industry and industrial development, and at the same time take due regard to regional and local policy considerations and other activities. (Section 1–2)

Furthermore, explicit legislative provisions enabled the state to regulate production schedules, postpone field development, and direct third-party access to facilities (NPD, 1996, section 4).

The center-right coalition government of Prime Minister Kjell Magne Bondevik examined the state of offshore affairs after winning the election in 2001 and issued a report to the Storting on offshore activities in 2002 (MPE, 2004). The report posited two scenarios for the NCS, 'decline' and 'long-term'. The decline scenario assumed the companies and the Norwegian state were satisfied to reap the rewards of past investments, allow the existing fields to decline (with oil production reduced to a trickle by 2020), and 'pursue policies which contribute to the relatively rapid phase-out of the oil and gas industry' (MPE, 2004, p. 8). While environmental interests would welcome such an outcome, the impact on employment, state revenues, work skills, technological development, foreign investment, and the international reach of Norwegian companies made the scenario unattractive to the government. By contrast, the long-term scenario assumed the industry and the state wished to recover much of the 60 percent of the crude oil remaining under the seabed, as well as the large amounts of recoverable gas (all together an extra 67 billion barrels of oil equivalent), 'to secure the best possible resource utilisation and the highest possible value creation for the Norwegian community' (MPE, 2004, pp. 8, 12). The MPE estimated that 'pursuing an aggressive policy to continue developing the petroleum sector' would result in 50 more years of oil and a century more of gas production (MPE, 2004, p. 9). The benefits of such a policy, according to the report, would be the continued funding of the welfare state and industrial policy, and the maintenance of 'leading-edge' technology with a global reach, while maintaining high health, safety, and environmental (HSE) standards. It wasn't much of a contest; the government, with broad support in the Storting, chose to pursue the long-term scenario in line with its mandate in the Ten Oil Commandments to consider social, economic, political, and environmental factors in the development of petroleum resources.

The Bondevik government identified four challenges to achieving the goals of the long-term scenario:

1. Increase recovery from existing fields,
2. Increase exploration activity,
3. Reduce the cost level on the NCS,
4. Further develop the competence of the Norwegian Petroleum Industry Cluster,

all the while continuing to lead the world in HSE safeguards.

To overcome these challenges, the government made several important commitments. First, as we saw in the section above, the MPE committed to a more aggressive licensing policy by offering significant amounts of new territory for exploration, while instituting a flexible approach to mature areas (which resulted in the creation of APA licenses). Second, the government pledged to reduce costs on the NCS by encouraging the use of advanced recovery techniques, coordinating the use of existing infrastructure, re-evaluating costly regulations, adjusting onshore supply facilities to serve offshore production more efficiently, and continuing to encourage and subsidize research and technology development in the petroleum sector. Third, the government committed to offshore tax reform (see the next section) to create incentives to explore for, develop, and extend production of oil and gas resources (MPE, 2004, pp. 3–6).

In typical Norwegian fashion, the government was not to force any of these initiatives on the offshore sector. In the early 2000s, KonKraft, a new cooperative forum, brought together industry and labor to discuss all aspects of offshore competitiveness (excluding labor contracts). Owned by the key organizations in the industry – including Offshore Norway, Norwegian Industry, the Norwegian Shipping Association, the Norwegian Business Association (NHO) and Norwegian Confederation of Trade Unions (LO, the primary labor organization) and its confederations *Fellesforbundet* and *Industri Energi* – KonKraft brought to the negotiating table the major players in the system from both industry and labor. Nordic corporatism, thus, provided the state with an organized set of interests committed to prolonging petroleum activity on the NCS. KonKraft offered the MPE advice on the streamlining of contracts, tax incentives, efficient technologies, and a host of other topics all aimed at decreasing exploration and production costs (KonKraft, 2023).

Advanced technology offered one path to maximizing petroleum recovery. The Norwegian state directed operators to incorporate improved oil recovery (IOR), enhanced oil recovery (EOR), and gas recovery techniques in their plans for development and operation (PDOs) that the MPE (and the Storting) had to approve before a deposit could be developed. PDOs, moreover, are not set in stone. As technology advances, field operators may wish to modify their production plans to take advantage of new recovery techniques. The MPE welcomed beneficial amendments, but as the ultimate offshore regulator, it also had the right to require operators to alter their PDOs when 'the authorities see a need for changes as a consequence of new knowledge about the deposit, new technology, commercial conditions or other factors that make such changes relevant' (MPE and Ministry of Labor and Social Inclusion, 2022, p. 14). Norway's early push to develop a world-class petroleum sector and to encourage collaboration between the companies, state officials, and research institutions to advance offshore technology was paying off (Enoksen, 2007).

Finally, as in any mature area, the NCS has become a complex network of production platforms, subsea well heads, processing facilities, and petroleum pipelines. Producing as much oil and gas as economically as possible requires cooperation among license holders operating in adjacent territories. Cooperation prevents duplicating equipment and services, which in turn requires the owners of infrastructure to lease to 'third parties' some part of their existing assets for usage fees. This 'third-party access' (TPA) to infrastructure, including pipelines, is governed by a separate set of rules referred to as the 'TPA Regulation', which sets tariffs for third-party use and overall principles for negotiations between operating groups. The MPE may use its deep knowledge of offshore activities to propose cooperative solutions involving TPA to operators looking to cut production costs. The Ministry also serves as the decider of last resort when negotiations between operators reach an impasse (Bjørnebye and Banet, 2019). Perhaps no policy illustrates better than this TPA policy the active role played by the Norwegian state in pursuing its offshore objectives.

We can illustrate this process by considering the case of Ekofisk in the North Sea. The original Ekofisk PDO in 1971 estimated the total recovery of petroleum from the field to be a very low 17 percent due to the field's complex chalk formations. The field's lifetime was estimated to be 25 years. Projected recovery from the field was raised in 1988 to 20–30 percent after the NPD approved a water injection plan in 1983 (Kvendseth, 1988; Norwegian

Petroleum, 2023a). In the early 1990s, Phillips sought to decommission parts of the Ekofisk field due to falling production and subsistence in the production facilities (Kvendseth, 1988). There were also concerns regarding the safety of Ekofisk due to subsidence and poor maintenance. Rather than accede to Phillips' request, the NPD instead directed the company to submit a revised PDO in 1994 resulting in the redevelopment of Ekofisk production facilities and the use of increased recovery techniques (Kvendseth, 1988). Phillips used water injection at Ekofisk W from 1989 until 2009 before shutting it down and replacing it with a subsea template. The NPD approved a new PDO for the development of Ekofisk South in 2011 and included production platform Ekofisk Z and subsea template Ekofisk VB for water injection. An amended PDO for an additional water injection template, Ekofisk VC, was approved in 2017 (Norwegian Petroleum, 2023a).

The employment of EOR technology at the end of Ekofisk's life will boost recovery from the field to more than 50 percent total reserves (Norwegian Petroleum, 2023a). The capacity of the Norwegian state to compel Phillips (since 2002, ConocoPhillips) and other private companies operating on the NCS has resulted in billions of barrels of extra oil produced from Ekofisk and other ageing North Sea fields.

Britain

British North Sea petroleum production declined steeply from the mid-2000s, steeper than the decline in Norway (see Figure 3.3, p. 59). Economic liberalization, which included divesting itself of its role in regulating the depletion of its North Sea petroleum resources, contributed to the decline. Without state intervention, companies were happy to take the low-hanging fruit then pick up stakes and leave the UKCS. As Gordon (2019, pp. 174–178) argues, the British approach to the UKCS lacked strategic direction, at least after the dismantling of the British National Oil Corporation (BNOC). The Department of Energy and Climate Change (DECC), now the Department of Business, Energy and Industrial Strategy (BEIS), had responsibility for regulating activities offshore just at a time when petroleum recovery became more complex in the mature North Sea. In addition, the Conservative government cut department budgets during a period of austerity following the economic crises of 2008–2010. Neglecting the offshore industry during this period could arguably be excused: the sector was much smaller relative to the economy than it was in Norway, and the transition away from fossil fuels was well underway (Gordon, 2019, p. 165). But the failure to attend to vital energy needs and potential financial benefits eventually caught up with British policy makers.

The rapid decline of UK petroleum production (especially natural gas) finally attracted the government's attention in the 2010s – about a decade after it did so in Norway. In 2013, the Tory Government under Prime Minister David Cameron announced a review of petroleum recovery efforts on the UKCS. Sir Ian Wood conducted the review and produced a report in 2014 subsequently known as the 'Wood Review' (Wood, 2014).

The Wood Review identified six key issues facing British policy makers: the need to

1. Maximize economic recovery for the UK (not just meet the commercial needs of the companies),
2. Ensure fiscal stability,
3. Establish a more effective offshore regulator,
4. Improve offshore asset stewardship,
5. Encourage greater collaboration between field operators,
6. Better implement industry strategies that affect the whole range of off-shore activities from exploration to decommissioning. (Wood, 2014, p. 5)

To meet these needs, the Review made four major recommendations:

1. Government (the Treasury and a new Regulator) and industry need to work together to develop and commit to a new strategy of MER UK.
2. Create a new regulatory body charged with the effective stewardship and regulation of the UKCS petroleum recovery, and to maximize collaboration across the industry.
3. Grant the regulator new powers, in addition to those already possessed by the authorities, to facilitate implementation of MER UK.
4. Develop and implement new sector strategies covering exploration, asset stewardship, regional development, infrastructure, technology, and decommissioning. (Wood, 2014, pp. 6–7)

The concept of 'maximizing economy recovery' on the UK continental shelf was not new. From the mid-1980s, the UK government described its policy as one of '*maximising the economic recovery of UK petroleum*' (Gallafent, Collier, and Jones, 2022, emphasis in original). At the time, the policy meant that individual companies on their individual fields should aim to maximize the recovery of petroleum in an economically efficient manner. This policy position shifted, and by 1993 the UK government had adopted a pre-tax approach to assessing the economic viability of remaining hydrocarbons irrespective of the actual division of realized value between licensees and the Exchequer (Gallafent, Collier, and Jones, 2022). In the early 2000s the government launched two initiatives to increase recovery rates, 'Fallow Areas' and 'Stewardship'. Fallow Areas encouraged licensees to surrender areas 'they were not actively exploring or producing from', while the Stewardship initiative sought to address underproduction from certain fields by, for instance, mediating intra-licensing group disagreements (Gordon, 2019, p. 178, n. 71). None of these strategies, however, amounted to a comprehensive solution to the problem of poor resource recovery in a declining province.

The Wood Review offered the UK government a comprehensive plan and it responded by implementing all the Wood recommendations through amendments to the *Petroleum Act 1998,* and two pieces of primary legislation, the *Infrastructure Act 2015* and the *Energy Act 2016.* Key to the new policy was a new Central Obligation, which was legally binding on all present and future parties operating on the UKCS: 'Relevant persons must, in the exercise of their relevant functions, take the steps necessary to secure that the maximum value of economically recoverable petroleum is recovered from the strata beneath relevant UK waters' (United Kingdom Government, nd, p. 4). Companies operating offshore were no longer free (on pain of penalty) to make decisions solely on commercial grounds, but were now required to collaborate with other companies in a manner that maximized the economic recovery of oil and gas from their own license area *and* from other license areas in their region of the UKCS.

With the implementation of the MER strategy on 18 March 2016, companies were legally obligated to take a cooperative and regional approach to offshore activity. According to the government's implementation strategy, companies were to prioritize maximum recovery in every aspect of petroleum mining. For instance, groups developing newly discovered deposits were required to work with nearby licensees to exploit existing infrastructure (often requiring third-party access) and plan new infrastructure suited to maximizing production from surrounding fields. In addition, companies were to keep abreast of technological developments and employ new recovery techniques as they became available. Decommissioning also required detailed analysis of a field's remaining resources and the possibility of additional recovery. Only when all other options were exhausted was the licensee authorized to abandon a field (United Kingdom Government, nd, pp. 4–6).

As the Wood Review made clear, an effective depletion policy required a new, muscular regulatory agency capable of deep intervention on the UKCS. The *Energy Act 2016* established the OGA, a new arms-length regulator, as a private company under the *Companies Act 2006* with the Secretary of State as the single shareholder. The OGA (which since March 2022 is now called the North Sea Transition Authority, NSTA) does not act on behalf of the Crown, nor are its members, officers, and staff regarded as Crown servants. It is, however, answerable to the Secretary of State and must implement the strategy decided by the political authorities. Effective implementation required expertise and funding adequate to the task, which the government noted characterized Norway's successful regulatory agency, the NPD (United Kingdom Government, nd, p. 14). Thus, to ensure stable and adequate funding (not dependent on government budgets), the government empowered the agency to collect annual levies from offshore companies.

The NSTA brings regulatory heft to the UKCS. It is subject to the same Central Obligation as every other offshore actor, but its primary responsibility is to support the MER UK strategy by working with industry to coordinate off-shore activities. The NSTA conducts licensing rounds, makes geological and other data available to companies, grants permissions for field development and decommissioning, enforces work programs, sits in on license holders' meetings, and mediates offshore disputes. It employs a range of incentives and sanctions, including notices, fines, and license revocation, to cajole resistant companies to agree to take certain actions.

The MER UK strategy adopted many of Norway's 'prudent production' requirements, including asset stewardship, optimization of production, third-party access, and the use of technology and innovation to maximize economic recovery. Prior to 2016 operators on the UKCS had free rein to use or abandon its assets as it saw fit. But implementation of the MER UK strategy brought change. Along with a new regulator with new powers and new objectives, operators were required to cooperate, collaborate, and maximize as companies had been doing on the NCS for several years. Thus, the implementation of the MER UK asset strategy brought about a reconvergence of Norway and the UK's depletion policies. Both aim to maximize recovery by encouraging cooperation among offshore companies and empowering their regulatory arms to harness the power of the state to alter company behavior when inconsistent with the aims of the government.

TAXATION

British and Norwegian petroleum tax policies continued to evolve after 1990, but they remained recognizable in both countries. The major difference was that while Norwegian governments strove to keep the tax regime relatively stable, British governments kept roiling the waters with frequent rate changes and new taxes.

Britain

In November 2022, Chief Executive Deirdre Michie of the Offshore Energies Association UK (OEUK), the successor to the United Kingdom Offshore Operators Association (UKOOA) and Britain's leading petroleum trade asso-ciation, decried the hefty increase in offshore taxes announced by Chancellor Jeremy Hunt: 'we remain proud to pay our taxes, but this latest increase means UK offshore operators will be paying a total rate of 75%. This rate is so high that it threatens to drive investment out of the UK altogether.... . But it's not just the rate that is so damaging. It's also the *disruption and uncertainty generated by constant changes to our tax system*' (OEUK, 2022b, emphasis added). It was a common complaint. In the eyes of offshore companies, the British offshore tax regime lacked predictability, which added additional uncertainty to the investment process. The smaller companies now active on the UKCS were especially vulnerable to changes in their tax liabilities.

The *Oil Tax Act 1975* established three sources of income for the Treasury: royalty payments, taxation on profits of petroleum production, and profit from state participation offshore. The end of state participation in the 1980s dried up the third source of revenue, and the elimination of all offshore royalty payments (a stable but regressive tax) after January 2003 dried up the first. That left taxes on profits as the remaining revenue stream for the Treasury (Gordon, 2019, p. 200). Two problems, however, plagued this tax from the Treasury's perspective. First, volatile petroleum prices made the Treasury uncertain. Revenues declined or stopped entirely when oil and gas prices fell, leaving little profit to tax. But when prices spiked, offshore companies reaped super-profits that could not be captured for the state using existing tax laws. Public pressure on the Treasury sometimes elicited changes to the tax regime that would then leave the offshore sector over-taxed when prices fell back thus causing companies to withhold investments. The second problem related to the increasing number of structures scheduled for decommissioning. Companies are allowed to claim back taxes paid years ago to help finance the tremendous cost of cleaning up and abandoning fields.

The British tax regime retained two legacy taxes from the early years and added others in the twenty-first century. The Petroleum Revenue Tax (PRT) and Ring-Fence Corporation Tax (RFCT) were the holdovers from the 1970s and 1980s. The PRT applies only to fields developed before 1993. At one time, the PRT was set at 75 percent and generated the lion's portion of government revenues from the UKCS. In 1993, the government set the rate at 50 percent, which lasted through 2015. In 2016, the government reduced the rate to 0 percent but did not abolish the tax so companies could continue to claim losses (including decommissioning costs) against previous PRT payments. The government created the RFCT in 1975 as the offshore version of corporate tax, initially set at the same rate as other corporate taxes, 20 percent. In 2008 the Labour government set the RFCT at a higher rate of 30 percent. The 'ring fence' provision prohibits companies from reducing their tax bill by applying losses from one development against profits from another. Each development is 'ring fenced' as a stand-alone entity.

In addition to the PRT and RFCT, the Labour government in 2002 decided to create a new Supplementary Charge (SC) – essentially an additional RFCT, minus allowances for financing costs and the 100 percent capital allowance allowed in the RFCT – to claw back the state windfall profits that accumulate when crude oil prices rise. The SC was initially set by Labour at 10 percent, went to 32 percent in 2011 under the Conservatives, then back down to 30 percent (2014), 20 percent (2015), and 10 percent (2016), all under the Tories (Gordon, 2019, pp. 200–204; Seely, 2023). The dramatic rise in oil and gas prices due in part to Russia's attack on Ukraine led the Tory government to seek relief for consumers by taxing offshore profits to offset rising household energy costs. To this end, Chancellor Rishi Sunak announced on 26 May 2022 the creation of an Energy Profits Levy (EPL) of 25 percent, which he hoped would satisfy calls for a windfall profits tax on petroleum income. The new tax would be temporary with an end date scheduled for 2025 (later extended to 31 March 2028). In addition, the Chancellor announced a new 'super deduction' designed to spark interest in UKCS investment. Companies, under this scheme, would receive an estimated 91.25 percent of their investment back in tax relief (Seely, 2023, p. 58). The reaction to the announcement was predictable. Labour congratulated the government for finally seeing the light. As the Shadow Chancellor Rachel Reeves commented, 'Labour welcomes the fact that the Government are finally acting on our calls to introduce a windfall tax' (Seely, 2023, p. 65). Some in the Conservative government agreed that the new tax looked like a Labour policy. Liz Truss, for instance, expressed her strong opposition to a windfall tax during her Tory leadership campaign and brief premiership stating: 'I am against a windfall tax. I believe it is the wrong thing to be putting companies off investing in the United Kingdom just when we need to be growing the economy' (Donaldson, 2022; Lawless, 2022). The offshore industry worried about profits, investment, and jobs, but did not put up a big fight. It was hard for the industry to resist a new tax when consumers were facing shocking energy bills. The new law received Royal Assent on 14 July 2022.

The introduction of the EPL brought the government's take from the UKCS from 40 percent to 75 percent, roughly the same as the Norwegian state's take (Seely, 2023, p. 78). But signs were that the new tax and the general instability of the tax system were discouraging investment on the UKCS, despite the massive incentives to spend money to save money going to taxes. The volatility of the UK offshore tax regime threatened to undercut the opening to investment inspired by MER.

Norway

In contrast to Britain, Norway maintained a stable, predictable offshore tax system for three decades. The ordinary company tax and the special tax remained the primary generators of offshore taxes. The government over 30 years has altered the rates on occasion, but the basic structure has remained constant. Tax reform in the 1990s, for instance, resulted in a reduction of the corporate tax rate in Norway to 28 percent (down from 50 percent). Consequently, the government increased the Special Petroleum Tax (SPT) from 35 to 50 percent bringing the total state tax take down from 85 percent to 78 percent. More recently, in 2022, the state offered companies temporary tax relief during COVID-19 (2020–2022), but also introduced a cash-flow based tax as part of the special tax to better ensure tax neutrality (i.e., a project profitable before tax is also profitable after tax) (Nyberg, Samuelsen, and Odland, 2022). The corporate rate currently stands at 22 percent and the SPT at 56 percent, but the total take remains 78 percent (Andal, 2023). While the top-level rates have remained steady, the government has more often fiddled with rules regarding deductions for exploration activities and onshore and offshore facility construction and operating expenses. Since the early 2000s the government has used the tax code to encourage exploration (especially for smaller companies) and reduce the differences in taxation between new entrants to the NCS and long-time operators (Gormley and Kristensen, 2019, pp. 83–87). Environmental groups have opposed some of these deductions as state subsidies that effectively undermine investment in renewable energy. To underline its point, a Norwegian organization called Bellona filed a complaint against the Norwegian tax authorities charging them with breaking the rules of the EEA Agreement. The European Free Trade Association (EFTA) Surveillance Agency ruled against Bellona in 2019 (Gormley and Kristensen, 2019, pp. 86–87).

Companies are also subject to additional offshore fees. As discussed in Chapter 3, royalty payments were eliminated for fields approved from 1 January 1987, but older fields were still required to pay. Area fees remain attached to licensees to encourage speedy exploration and relinquishment of unused territory back to the state.

New offshore taxes have come in the form of environmental fees that are not designed to raise revenues but to meet international commitments to reduce harmful emissions. To help reduce the release of greenhouse gases, Norway implemented a carbon tax system in 1991, which is set for 2023 at NOK 1.78 per standard cubic meter of gas and NOK 2.03 per liter of oil or condensate (Norwegian Tax Administration, 2023). The tax is designated in the petroleum tax formula as a deductible operating expense. Norwegian authorities have exempted operators with functioning CO_2 capture systems from the carbon tax to encourage innovative offshore ventures. Currently, two fields, Sleipner and Snøhvit, have commercially viable projects that capture CO_2 from natural gas processing and reinject it into dedicated storage sites (International Energy Agency, 2020).

As a signatory to the 1999 Gothenburg Protocol to Abate Acidification, Eutrophication and Ground-level Ozone, Norway is committed to reducing nitrogen oxide (NOx), a main cause of smog, poor air quality, and acid rain.

Sources of NOx include offshore and onshore gas flares. To combat NOx emissions, the Norwegian authorities imposed a nitrogen oxide tax in 2007. In response to an industry concerned about additional costs, the government and representatives of the offshore sector (as well as coastal shipping and aviation groups) negotiated the creation of a NOx Fund that would help the government meet its international obligations, while alleviating some of the added financial burden on offshore developments (Gormley and Kristensen, 2019, pp. 87–88). Companies that join the Fund pay an annual fee that is less than they would pay in nitrogen oxide tax (set for 2023 at NOK 24.46 per kilogram, up from NOK 21.94 in 2018). The Fund then uses this money for NOx emission reduction measures. If the Fund fails to reach its reduction goals, the tax is reimposed (Bektas, et al., nd). The system has clearly succeeded: Norway has met its emission targets, industry has developed cost-effective technologies to reduce NOx, and groups such as the Environmental Defense Fund are pressuring the UK to adopt a similar system (Bektas, et al., nd, pp. 1–2).

PARTICIPATION

On the surface, state offshore participation policies in Britain and Norway in the early 2020s looked similar to their 1990 versions. The British state did not re-enter the UKCS as an owner – despite 13 years of Labour government – while the Norwegian state remained a major investor and participant offshore. But beneath the surface, much had changed, especially in Norway. Offshore systems of participation remained different on the two continental shelves, but the differences had narrowed considerably. There were signs of convergence.

The most important changes to participation arrangements were made in Norway, and mostly concerned Statoil. As we recounted in Chapter 3, Statoil had undergone a 'wing-clipping' in the mid-1980s. The state's share of offshore fields was now divided between Statoil and the State's Direct Financial Interest (SDFI), which Statoil operated on behalf of the state. Statoil continued in its role as monopoly seller of natural gas produced on the NCS. But several developments in the late 1980s and 1990s increased pressure on the government to restructure further its petroleum interests. First, the wave of liberalization and privatization that washed over Britain under Margaret Thatcher lapped the shores of Norway as well. Statoil was the last of the large state-owned oil companies in Europe to remain entirely in government hands; market-oriented politicians, on principle, called for its privatization. Second, Statoil leadership felt constrained by its ownership structure. Its ability to take commercial risks, raise capital, expand overseas, and compete for contracts was limited by its responsibility to the state as a tool of government policy. Some pressure had been relieved by the 1985 reforms, but limitations remained. Third, oil prices were very low in the late 1980s and slumped again in the 1990s challenging Statoil's profitability. Finally, the EEA Agreement and the Hydrocarbon Directive prohibited the government from explicitly favoring Statoil; the company would have to compete for licenses like any other private company (Gormley and Kristensen, 2019, p. 70). Statoil would need to get commercially fit.

Statoil recognized early its need for greater freedom and significant additional resources to become a global petroleum powerhouse. Company leaders began lobbying strongly for partial privatization and a greater share of the income from the state's holdings in the SDFI as early as 1990. The Labour government, however, shut down the discussion in 1992. Statoil CEO Harald Norvik reopened the dialogue in January 1999 with a controversial speech to the Norwegian Petroleum Society calling for a restructuring of Norway's petroleum industry. Opponents of privatization criticized him for overstepping his bounds, but he articulated what many politicians and civil servants had been reticent to say (Eide, nd-a). To achieve his goal, Norvik had to win over the Labour party and the unions. He spent much time cultivating Labour's deputy leader Jens Stoltenberg and Yngve Hågensen, the director of the LO. And it paid off. By early 2000 the Labour party was ready to back a less radical restructuring plan than the one put forward by Norvik and his successor Olav Fjell. But it did include the sale of part of Statoil to private shareholders and the transfer of a significant portion of SDFI back to the company to provide additional financial muscle. Some significant Labour resistance remained, but Stoltenberg took over as Prime Minister in March 2000 and won full party backing of the reform plan in November. The Storting passed the legislative package in April 2001 (Eide, nd-a).

The changes, eventually agreed, represented a compromise between the Statoil leadership, which pushed for maximum privatization and transferred interests from SDFI, and the state, which was not willing to cede complete control. In the end, one-third of Statoil's value was listed as shares on the Oslo and New York stock exchanges on 18 June 2001. In addition, Statoil purchased 15 percent and Norsk Hydro (and other companies) 6.5 percent of SDFI from the state.[1] The bulk of the state's offshore interests (roughly a third of offshore reserves) were then placed under the management of a new state-owned company called Petoro, founded on 9 May 2001 (Eide, nd-a; Gormley and Kristensen, 2019, p. 71). Petoro is not another oil company, but rather a financial management company whose sole responsibility is to manage the Norwegian government interest in oil and gas fields on the NCS. The company, with its small staff, participates in offshore consortia and votes

---

[1]   In 2007 Statoil and Norsk Hydro merged their oil and gas divisions briefly becoming StatoilHydro until returning to Statoil in 2009.

the state's share (it reports to the Minister), but does not participate in licensing rounds and cannot become an operator.[2] Its purpose 'is to ensure maximum value and achieve the highest possible income to the State from SDFI' (Petoro, nd). State participation is thus solely profit-driven, if by 'profit' we mean maximum return on public investment.

Statoil was no longer a policy tool or 'national champion'. The company stood separated from the state's participatory interests. True, the state remained a majority shareholder, but Statoil was operating on a commercial basis committed to maximizing shareholder value, full stop. One of the shareholders just happened to be the Norwegian state. Statoil's new global freedom eventually allowed it to refocus its mission. In 2018 the company changed its name to Equinor to reflect its transformation from a state oil and gas company to a public-private energy enterprise. The corporation would remain a petroleum producer, but would also invest heavily in technologies to reduce greenhouse gas emissions from the production of hydrocarbons and in renewable sources of energy such as wind. Green investments, however, could not hide the fact that the enterprise continued to make the bulk of its money by producing carbon-based energy.

The state's restructuring of its interests in the offshore sector required altering public participation in the gas transportation network, the world's largest (Bjørnebye and Banet, 2019, p. 114). The implementation of the EU's Gas Market Directive of 1998 put in jeopardy the Gas Negotiating Committee (GFU), formed in 1986 (see Chapter 3). The GFU, as the sole seller of Norwegian gas, fell afoul of EEA competition rules leaving it open to a suit filed by the European Commission in 2001 charging the companies (Statoil and Norsk Hydro) with price fixing (Eide, nd-b). In December 2001 the parties announced a settlement that effectively opened the Norwegian gas market. The state disbanded the GFU and allowed each gas producer to sell on the open market (Lindroos, et al., 2002). This liberalization of the Norwegian gas industry, coupled with regulated third-party access to the Norwegian gas transport network, brought the EEA much closer to a true single European market in gas, but left Norwegian authorities without familiar policy levers.

---

[2]   For example, when selecting the consortia members for the Ormen Lange field in 2009, the Norwegian government selected Statoil (25.3%), Shell (17.8%), PGNiG Upstream (14%) and Vår (6.3%). It also awarded 36.4% to Petoro as the SDFI (NPD, 2023d). This large share was based on the knowledge that Ormen Lange was likely to contain vast amounts of gas, and therefore it was in the Norwegian state's interest to own a large share. As a result of the 36% stake in the field, the Norwegian government receives 36% of the profits from the field, in addition to the tax revenues from the gas sales.

To regain some control of the gas network, the government created two new companies that conformed to EEA rules. Gassco was founded in 2001 as a fully state-owned company charged with operating the vast pipeline and processing system delivering gas from offshore fields to Britain and the continent, as well as LNG to global customers. The second company, Gassled, was established in 2003 as a partnership comprised of Statoil, Petoro and several private companies, an arrangement that gave the state a controlling interest in the joint venture. Gassled owns the gas processing and transport facilities and employs Gassco to operate them. Both companies meet the competition requirements of the EEA, but allow Norwegian authorities to manage the transportation network as a neutral party prioritizing efficiency, safety, and sustainability.

Recently, the Norwegian government has notified the private companies partnering in Gassled that it intends to purchase their assets at the end of their concession period, which for most is 2028. The state, in effect, is nationalizing the gas transportation network and processing facilities (Geiger, 2023). In 2022, Norway supplied the EU and UK with about 25 percent of their combined natural gas demand. This makes the NCS the primary source of gas for Europe after Russia's supply dried up due to sanctions and sabotage (of the Nord Stream pipelines). The gas network has become a strategic priority for Norway and may account for the government's decision. The companies and the Progress party have raised objections, but the opposition to the decision seems muted at best.

Finally, we end this section with a word about Norway's Oil Fund (officially Government Pension Fund Global), the world's largest sovereign wealth fund, which is valued at approximately $1.5 trillion and controls, on average, 1.5 percent of every publicly traded company in the world. The government established it in 1990 after the Willoch government's Skånland Commission recommended it as a defense against volatile oil prices and a flood of economically destabilizing petrodollars (see Chapter 3). The Fund's mission is to take in money generated by petroleum activities and invest the surpluses in assets outside Norway. The sources of income include the large amounts generated by the SDFI, as well as license fees, taxes, and Equinor dividends. Norges Bank Investment Management (established in 1998) – part of the Norwegian Central Bank – manages the investment fund on behalf of the Ministry of Finance. In 2001 the Storting limited the state to taking 4 percent of the Fund to help source its annual budget. The policy represents a national consensus around the idea that profits from petroleum production in this generation must be saved to promote the welfare of future generations (Center for Public Impact, 2019).

RECONVERGENCE

By the early 2020s, two offshore models that had looked very different in 1990 had now reconverged in significant ways (see Figure 4.1). Both British and Norwegian North Sea provinces had reached maturity and were in danger of being abandoned before being depleted. The two countries also possessed promising but difficult frontier areas they wanted explored. Thus, officials in both countries recognized the need to coordinate private offshore activities to extract the last commercially viable oil and gas from the North Sea, while enticing companies into riskier petroleum provinces. The discretionary licensing systems in each country provided the tools needed to open their provinces to leaner, hungrier companies looking for 'table scraps' and to force larger companies to employ their considerable resources to efficiently scrub an area before abandoning it. Slight differences existed between the two licensing systems, but both sets of regulators pursued a fixed goal – maximum extraction – using a flexible approach. In this system of 'flexible coercion' state officials offer companies the freedom to innovate, but as overseers of their provinces on behalf of their people, they will not hesitate to force companies to take actions for the common good (i.e., for the petroleum industry, shelf geology, and domestic society). Discretionary systems also allow regulators to offer effective sweeteners to companies willing to explore for petroleum in risky waters. The UK has employed this strategy to positive effect. Environmental interests and political parties with strong green commitments, however, have stymied Norwegian attempts to explore further north. A change of government would probably remove the political block and bring Norway back in line with the UK.

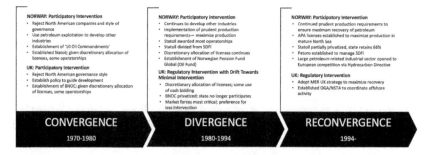

Figure 4.1   Variation of intervention regime since 1970

International commitments have also resulted in a convergence of systems. The EU's Hydrocarbon Directive forced both Britain and Norway to open their discretionary process to public scrutiny and eliminate protectionist elements in their licensing criteria. Both countries adopted public criteria for awarding licenses, which limited but did not eliminate the discretionary aspect of the licensing process. After decades of encouraging global petroleum companies to favor national suppliers, state authorities dropped 'buy local' requirements and liberalized their offshore supply industries. Norway also had to drop its favoritism toward Norwegian oil and gas companies in the licensing process, which contributed to the decision to privatize part of Statoil.

In terms of licensing, depletion policy, and even taxation – where the UK's relatively unstable petroleum system still looked similar to Norway's – the British state was shifting most toward a more directed regulatory system, at least where it was not limited by the EU. But Britain was not moving toward state participation on the UKCS; there was no talk of reviving BNOC. Reconvergence regarding participation would have to mean Norway moving away from state ownership of offshore enterprises. What we have seen, of course, is not a removal of the Norwegian state as an offshore owner. State equity ownership on the NCS has remained significant. What has changed is the state's decision to refrain from using its participation in consortia as a policy tool to affect depletion rates, research and development, or regional employment. The state uses its SDFI as an information window into the consortia operating on the NCS and uses its votes and investments to support its interests, which the state has defined in commercial terms. Moreover, it is happy to allow Petoro and Equinor to make money without burdening them with a policy role. The licensing and regulatory structure provide Norwegian officials the tools they need to implement policy decisions. The caveat to this conclusion is the proposed nationalization of the gas transportation network. How the state will use its ownership of the network will not be known until at least the end of the decade.

The North Sea system contains two models, the British and Norwegian. The two models have converged in important ways, as we have seen in this chapter. Both have adopted offshore regulatory regimes where states not only set the rules, but also direct the traffic. The state plays an active role in coordinating the activities of private companies across the entire petroleum province. But the two countries have not converged so much that they have adopted the same intervention regime. State participation still sets Norway apart from Britain's policy of regulatory intervention. Norway's participatory regime has edged closer to the regulatory model by promising not to use participation in offshore enterprises as a tool to achieve policy goals – for now. In fact, state participation remains a powerful coercive instrument should the government find the need to use it. In sum, British and Norwegian offshore policies have indeed converged, but they have not merged. The British model remains regulatory, the Norwegian, participatory.

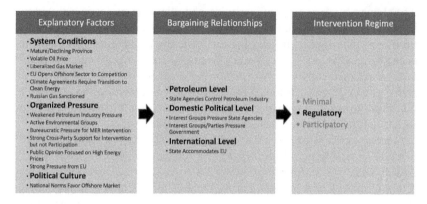

Figure 4.2   Reconvergence: Great Britain

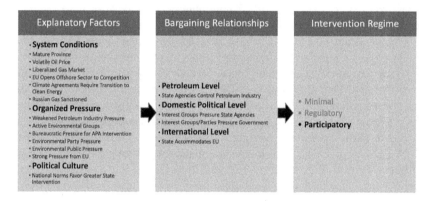

Figure 4.3   Reconvergence: Norway

How do we explain the reconvergence (see Figures 4.2 and 4.3)? Four causes stand out. First, both petroleum provinces entered their mature phase in the twenty-first century. Prodding companies to produce the last available petroleum out of the ground required centralized coordination, regulatory coercion, and financial incentives. Both states embraced their new role with gusto. Second, membership in the EEA required Britain and Norway to relinquish state discretion to market forces in some areas. The prohibition against playing favorites in licensing eliminated the ability to guarantee work for national and regional champions in the petroleum and offshore supplies sectors. Furthermore, the loss of licensing discretion raised additional questions about the usefulness of a state-owned petroleum company the government could no longer favor. Third, policy makers and the public alike realized that the prevention of global warming required an energy transition from fossil fuels to renewables and carbon capture. Governments made international pledges to reduce greenhouse gasses, but the transition would still require large quantities of hydrocarbons for the foreseeable future. Publics expected governments to take an active role in managing energy resources, but disagreement existed over how far the state should go. Some, of course, believed that the government's role was to ban the exploration for new sources of petroleum, or more radically, end the production of oil and gas altogether (see Chapter 5). But this was a minority view; most were looking for an orderly transition. Finally, the virtual end to Russian oil and gas supplies across most of Europe disrupted the energy market, sent prices soaring, and cast fear into the hearts of European citizens. Europeans were looking to their political leaders to keep the energy flowing at a reasonable price. Taken together, these developments pushed in the direction of strong government control.

The bargaining relationships were similar in both countries. At the petroleum level, state agencies had the information, expertise, and policy tools they needed to maximize production in a mature area. Greater diversity of producers on both shelves also meant the biggest players of the past, the international oil companies (IOCs), saw their influence diluted. At the domestic political level, state agencies could resist most interest group pressure and since petroleum policy was not generally a top concern of voters – unless retail prices spiked as they did in 2022 – governments could hold off the demands of political parties channeling interest group pressure for policy change. Aside from temporarily subsidizing fuel prices and raising windfall taxes (in the UK), the parties had no reason to change petroleum policies. The one exception was in Norway, where the Socialist Left's insistence on banning exploration in Norway's north suggested that parties are still important to petroleum policymaking. It is also a reminder that democratic governance stands behind the state's control of offshore activities.

Finally, the international level was dominated not by OPEC, as in the past, but by the directives from the EU, via the EEA, and the EEA's adjudication process. The opening of the licensing system and the liberalization of the gas market (by dismantling the GFU) and the offshore supplies market weakened the ability of British and Norwegian authorities to favor domestic economic interests, a major goal of both countries from the beginning. In some ways this development took the North Sea system back to the early days of minimal offshore regulation. The difference, however, is that both countries have built up significant domestic capacities in every aspect of petroleum exploration and development – and no longer need the state's support. They are well-placed to compete in the global market for offshore services.

5. Future: transitioning to a clean energy province

The North Sea system of petroleum production started as a bare framework for bringing order to a rush for offshore black gold. Over the course of six decades, the British and Norwegian states built the legal, bureaucratic, and financial capacity to shape offshore activities to meet onshore needs. State officials adapted their offshore systems to changing energy markets, global political conditions, and domestic attitudes toward states and markets while keeping some of the biggest private enterprises in the world relatively happy. The offshore dance of agencies and companies has not always been graceful; plenty of toes have been crushed, and tragically, lives lost. But the system, as it has evolved in both countries, has proved responsive, flexible, and resilient. It has also proved profitable for offshore companies and the British and Norwegian peoples. Viewed from a distance, the North Sea system is an example of good governance.

What does the future hold? We do not expect wholesale changes to systems that parliaments and state agencies have fine-tuned for decades, but major changes are shaking global energy markets and Britain and Norway will have to adapt, again. Offshore licensing, taxation, and state participation will have to adjust to the long-term consequences of a sanctioned Russia prevented from supplying Europe with cheap gas and the slow-motion *revolution* euphemistically called the 'energy transition'. Europe both needs fossil fuels and must eliminate fossil fuels. The dilemma is reshaping the politics of energy in Britain, Norway, Europe, and the world. Our explanatory framework helps us understand how all of this will affect state intervention on the British and Norwegian shelves.

FOUR OPTIONS

As we have argued throughout the book, understanding offshore state intervention regimes requires an analysis of the system conditions, organized pressures, and political culture that affect bargaining relationships in the policymaking process. State intervention in the form of regulation, taxation, and participation increases when system conditions favor state control; the strongest interests pressure government to intervene, and the national political culture is more dirigiste than liberal. These factors affect the bargaining strength of the state over the petroleum companies resulting in a more interventionist regime.

Many system conditions will remain relatively unchanged. State capacity in the form of petroleum sector information, legal powers, and bureaucratic competence will persist in both countries. The mature North Sea provinces will continue their gradual decline, but will compete for companies willing to invest in small deposits buried in complex geological formations. High-cost frontier areas will stay underdeveloped until petroleum prices rise high enough to justify production and further exploration. That could happen if Western sanctions on Russian oil and gas are made more effective and wide-spread, or Russian domestic instability undermines its capacity to produce and export petroleum. In that case, Europe will expect Britain and Norway to squeeze as much oil and gas as possible from their continental shelves. Norway will, of course, remain energy independent, but the War in Ukraine and the destruction of the German-Russian Nord Stream pipeline system in the Baltic Sea has revealed vulnerabilities to nefarious state actors (and possibly well-financed non-state actors) willing and able to destroy offshore petroleum production and transport facilities. Norway's security jitters are exacerbated by Europe's dependence on Norwegian gas. A security failure in Norway will have disastrous consequences for its North Atlantic Treaty Organization (NATO) allies and European Economic Area (EEA) partners on the continent. Britain is a net importer of petroleum, but as a major NATO power and significant contributor to Ukraine's military efforts, it too must take seriously the security challenges in the North Sea. Taken together, these system conditions will certainly not encourage Britain and Norway to lessen state control offshore and may well push both states to greater intervention in the name of national security.

Political pressures in each country will likely look similar in the short term, but differences may emerge by the end of the decade. The petroleum companies operating on both continental shelves are subject to stringent regulation, but they understand the system, enjoy open lines of communication with regulators, and take advantage of the flexibility built into the current licensing system. They will always complain about high taxes, but politicians seem to have learned when to take these complaints seriously and when to dismiss them as noise. More serious pressure, however, is likely to come from environmental interest groups, especially as we get closer to 2030 when most European countries plan to have reduced carbon emissions by at least 40 percent (using a 1990 baseline) and 2050, the target for full carbon neutrality. The pressure on governments to halt hydrocarbon production and usage is only likely to grow. The effectiveness of this pressure will probably be more apparent in Norway than Britain. Britain's two-party system tends to dilute strong interest group pressure because the Conservative and Labour parties are large coalitions of interests. Currently, the Conservative party does not look exposed to takeover by radical environmental groups, but the Labour party is more vulnerable, as we will see below. Norway's fragmented party system is much more vulnerable than the British to pressure groups that can capture small but key parties (as we saw in Chapter 4). The Norwegian Socialist Left party threatened to bring the Labour-led coalition government down if the Ministry of Petroleum and Energy (MPE) did not refrain from issuing new licenses on the northern Norwegian Continental Shelf (NCS). The state's strong interest in developing remaining deposits on the Norwegian shelf for financial and security purposes is soon to clash with a strong anti-carbon movement that seeks to end the apparent policy contradiction of a country committed to both decarbonization and petroleum exports in favor of the former (Milne, 2023).

Changes in system conditions and organized pressures could alter some of the bargaining relationships that influence the intervention regime. State agencies and petroleum companies will not see much change in their relationships; the state and the private sector will continue to work closely to manage declining provinces. But domestic political relations could be altered if environmental interest groups and public opinion turn strongly against hydrocarbon production due to the felt effects of climate change. Governments would have to respond. And so might the European Union (EU) or other multilateral groups. Brexit took away a source of multilateral pressure on the United Kingdom (UK), but it will probably have to enter a tighter relationship with the EU that may have some impact on the offshore sector. Norway will remain a member of the EEA and could be subject to deep cuts in hydrocarbon production if the EU takes a collective decision to move faster toward carbon neutrality.

The interplay of these factors will result in each country adopting one of four options (see Table 5.1).

1. Option 1: Maximum Recovery, Regulatory Regime
    This is the status quo option for Britain. State agencies remain deeply involved in the regulation and coordination of private enterprises operating offshore. The aim is maximum production as quickly as possible for as long as possible. Choosing this option assumes demand for oil and gas will continue for at least as long as the continental shelf contains recoverable reserves. It also assumes climate goals can be met by the rapid expansion of clean energy sources and the use of carbon capture. Choosing this option assumes that all major policy goals can be achieved without state participation offshore.
2. Option 2: Maximum Recovery, Participatory Regime
    This is the status quo option for Norway. High production remains the primary goal offshore under this scenario, but state participation is also desired. Security could be one driver of participatory intervention. The

military situation in the North Sea and North Atlantic could deteriorate to the point where political leaders, backed by public opinion, feel it prudent to take control of a strategic industry by introducing participation (Britain), increasing the level or functional use of participation (Norway), or nationalizing all or most of the offshore sector. An expansion of the War in Ukraine to neighboring countries, the use of nuclear weapons, or the sabotage of offshore transit or production systems could prompt such a response. So could a withdrawal of the US from NATO, leaving the North Atlantic unprotected. Climate change could be another driver of participation, which could be used to press forward the development of alternative energy sources, perhaps financed by profits from the sale of oil and gas.

3. Option 3: Production Phase Out, Regulatory Regime
   Policy makers will likely choose this option if environmental groups capture important political parties and convince the public that climate change goals cannot be met unless petroleum is phased out quickly. The onset of severe weather events clearly tied to climate change might motivate the public to demand an end to petroleum production. Alternatively, a technical breakthrough on clean energy production, possibly in nuclear fusion or in the use of hydrogen, could make hydrocarbons obsolete. Choosing this option would require officials to use existing policy tools such as licensing and taxation to encourage field abandonment. Instead of maximizing recovery, policy makers would restrict it as much as possible without breeching their licensing agreements. No new licenses would be offered on any part of the continental shelf.

4. Option 4 Production Phase Out, Participatory Regime
   This option assumes the scenario outlined in Option 3, but officials pursue abandonment with greater urgency. Instead of waiting for the licensing process to take its course, the state orders the appropriation of offshore holdings and halts production. The option is drastic but realistic if environmental groups gain significant influence.

Britain and Norway currently pursue Options 1 (Britain) and 2 (Norway). One or both of the countries could choose alternative options. Both states have the capacity and experience to choose any of the four options if they wish.

LICENSING

The licensing systems on both continental shelves offer state officials all the tools they need to meet depletion targets. The reforms of the 1970s gave agencies the right to regulate offshore depletion in the national interest (see Chapter 2). Experience demonstrated that limiting depletion during the pro-

Table 5.1   Strategy options and intervention regimes

| | | Intervention Regime | |
		Regulatory	Participatory
Depletion Strategy	**Max. Recovery**	Maximum, Regulatory Option 1	Maximum, Participatory Option 2
	Phase Out	Phase Out, Regulatory Option 3	Phase Out, Participatory Option 4

duction phase of a field, although possible, undermined relations with offshore companies. Both states chose not to use their regulatory power to discourage production, but the right to do so remains.

Britain's Maximize Economic Recovery (UK) (MER UK) strategy and the Innovate licenses, and Norway's Pre-Defined Area (APA) licensing system reflect the two countries' mutual goal of maximizing production from their North Sea sectors. According to the NPD (2023c), Norway has produced a little over half of its recoverable reserves (52 percent) and predicts a high level of activity on the NCS for the next 50 years. Britain has produced possibly two-thirds of its recoverable reserves giving it about 30 more years of production (OEUK, 2022a). If maximum extraction is the goal, the licensing systems will not appreciably change; they give the state control and the companies flexibility.

But all of this could – and is perhaps likely – to change. We see hints of change in Norway already. The delay of the 26th licensing round to at least 2025 due to Socialist Left objections could significantly slow or completely halt exploration for deposits north of 62°N. Add any restrictions on APA licenses and Norway will have embraced Option 4 (Production Phase Out, Participatory Regime) and started a phased shutdown of the NCS. Norwegian groups committed to ending petroleum production – including Greenpeace Norway, Friends of the Earth Norway, WWF-Norway, *Natur og Ungdom*, and the Bellona Foundation – have increased pressure on the state. The groups oppose all petroleum production, but they are especially concerned about licensing in the frigid, fragile, largely unexplored Barents Sea. Opposing these groups are several international oil companies (IOCs), dreaming of big undiscovered deposits, and the pragmatic elements of the Labour government that see new discoveries as welcome help for a Europe eager to fill the energy void left by sanctioned Russia (Meredith, 2023).

Britain also has environmental groups opposed to offshore petroleum production (see Chapter 4). Their influence is strongest in the Labour party. If elected, Labour promises to halt the issuing of new oil and gas licenses (Walker, 2023). Existing and approved fields would not be affected, nor would any licenses awarded in the 33rd Round (2023) by the Conservative government. The offshore industry would remain viable for several decades longer, but the effect of a licensing ban would signal to hydrocarbon producers that their services will soon no longer be needed – unless they turn their energies to producing clean power. A Labour government would not be the first to shut down its petroleum licensing system for environmental reasons. Denmark, France, and Ireland, much smaller producers, have already halted new licensing and have gone further by pledging a managed phaseout of all petroleum production through a multilateral organization called the Beyond Oil and Gas Alliance (BOGA) (BOGA, 2023). Labour has not suggested it would make such a commitment, but pressure from environmental groups will certainly open the conversation. Such a policy would effectively end the MER UK strategy, which environmentalists have tried unsuccessfully to halt through the courts (Keating, 2022; Nasralla, 2022). It would also require a rewriting of the 1998 *Petroleum Act* (Bridge and Weszkalnys, 2023). Should Labour take power and move to enact a license ban and a phasedown of production, oil companies and organized labor – in a rare display of common purpose – will rally against the elimination of an economic sector by government fiat. The party may find it advantageous to take its time coming up with a plan, which is likely to be a compromise that extends offshore activity longer than anti-petroleum groups would like. Even if a new government does change offshore policy, it can always be reversed by a returning Tory government, although restarting a policy after dismantling significant state capacity in a sector is difficult. In any case, the licensing system under Labour is not likely to change very much, only put to a new purpose.

Licensing for oil and gas production may not survive much longer on the British and Norwegian shelves, but licensing for green technologies is just getting started. Both countries offer licenses to build offshore wind farms, either fixed or floating. In Britain, the *Energy Act 2004* vested the right to grant offshore wind licenses to the Crown Estate[1] (BVG Associates, 2019). By 2008, the country was the largest producer of offshore wind power generation. The Crown Estate has conducted four rounds of licensing with over 40 wind farms now operating offshore. Norway has been slow to establish an offshore wind licensing regime, but it has now conducted one licensing round (2023) for two designated areas in the North Sea. Some licenses were awarded by auction, others by discretion (BAHR, 2022). Offshore wind power generation will be a growth area in Norway.

---

[1]   The Crown Estate belongs to the British monarch, but is operated as a corporation governed by a board of commissioners acting on behalf of the King. The entity collects lands and holdings that generate revenues passed directly to the Treasury. Scotland's holdings are managed by the Crown Estate Scotland.

Offshore hydrogen production is also in the planning stages. Britain's North Sea Transition Authority (NSTA) has joined with several private companies to begin planning the Bacton Energy Hub (off the coast of Norfolk), an extensive network of on and offshore facilities to produce and store hydrogen. Hydrogen produced by wind generated electricity (green hydrogen) can be stored in depleted offshore gas fields, while methane from producing gas fields can be used as feedstock for hydrogen production (blue hydrogen) with the emitted CO_2 stored beneath the seabed in a carbon capture scheme. The planned system uses existing offshore infrastructure to produce and transport hydrogen (FuelCellsWorks, 2022). A similar system called the Acorn Hydrogen Project is planned for offshore Scotland (Acorn, 2023). Norway is playing catch up to Britain regarding hydrogen. The government is not yet convinced that producing hydrogen is environmentally or economically viable since the conversion of one source of energy to another source results in a loss of energy (Tomasgard and Durakovic, 2023). But if Europe moves toward a hydrogen-based economy – as seems likely, especially for hard-to-electrify planes and ships – Norway may find demand for hydrogen outstripping demand for gas. In early 2023, Equinor and the German energy company RWE signed a memorandum of understanding (MOU) committing the two companies to working together on large developments needed for Germany and the EU to make the transition to green energy, including hydrogen. The MOU constitutes a start for Norway (Buljan, 2023).

Finally, both Britain and Norway have begun issuing licenses for carbon capture and storage (CCS) on the continental shelves. Unlike petroleum, which is valued by a global market, carbon has little market value. Storing it is not rational unless governments artificially raise the price of emitting CO_2 to the point of financial pain. Governments can then relieve that pain by offering companies credits for carbon storage. Norway's NOx Fund operates on the same principle (see Chapter 4). Both Britain and Norway have the technological capacity and offshore infrastructure to facilitate the reversal of carbon flow in the North Sea. Carbon has now started flowing back beneath the seabed, often to replace the carbon that once flowed up.

Norway began CCS operations before they were fashionable. For two decades the NCS had the only two CCS operations in Europe. Since 1996, approximately one million metric tons of CO_2 produced from the Sleipner gas field has been separated, captured, and reinjected into sub-sea formations. A similar process has been going on since 2008 in the far north where CO_2 from Snøvit is reinjected (MPE, 2023). In late 2020, the Storting approved an ambitious CCS development project called Longship (MPE, 2020), part of which is the development of a CO_2 transportation and storage network christened 'Northern Lights' (operated jointly by Equinor, Shell, and Total) (MPE, 2023). In 2022, Northern Lights signed the first CCS contract for CO_2

transportation across an international border with the Dutch company Yara. The first deliveries should begin in 2025. The MPE has awarded six licenses, since 2022, to companies seeking to explore offshore areas for suitable storage sites. So far, the MPE has conducted two rounds. Like the petroleum system, licenses are awarded by discretion based on the qualifications of the companies and the proposed workplans (NPD, 2022a).

In Britain, the NSTA launched its first carbon capture licensing round in June 2022 (Skopljak, 2023). The 20 licenses on offer attracted 26 bids from 19 players (Cavcic, 2022). In 2023, the NSTA awarded all 20 licenses to 12 companies, which will still need to secure access to the seabed through The Crown Estates or Crown Estates Scotland. The carbon capture system enabled by these licenses could, by 2030, store up to 30 million metric tons of CO_2 per year, approximately 30 percent of the UK's current annual production (NSTA, 2023).

TAXATION

Norway's offshore tax regime is stable and predictable, if costly to the producers (see Chapter 4). Britain's remains volatile – and not always beneficial. The 2022 windfall tax take, for instance, dropped 40 percent in early 2023 due to the fall in oil prices, making its collection hardly worth the trouble. Experts criticized the government for implementing a badly designed tax that undermined industry confidence and yielded very little revenue (Pickard and Sheppard, 2023). The Conservative government responded to the companies with some minor tweaks, but Labour doubled down with a pledge to backdate the tax to the start of 2022 and end substantial investment allowances.

The British tax system has also come under pressure from environmental activists. Paid to Pollute, an activist group backed by Greenpeace, Uplift, and Friends of the Earth, announced a high court challenge to the government's offshore tax system in December 2021. The group argued that the tax system effectively acts as a public subsidy for offshore activities by offering tax relief for offshore development and decommissioning. The government argued that tax deductions were not the same as subsidies and that no public money was supporting private companies (McKie, 2021). The court ruled against the claimants in January 2022 (Thomas, 2022).

The British and Norwegian offshore tax systems are likely to survive legal challenges. Parliaments, however, could be less sympathetic to the status quo than courts. Governments intent on speeding the unwinding of offshore petroleum production could use the tax system to discourage new development and make existing fields unsustainable. Seemingly small changes in the structure of tax allowances can impact decisions on field development, enhanced recovery methods, and decommissioning. Without much effort, both parliaments could quietly reform the tax system and drive producers off the continental shelves.

STATE PARTICIPATION

Britain and Norway are both committed to maximum resource recovery on the continental shelf. The two North Sea nations, however, have taken different approaches to state participation. Could that change? Perhaps. The energy transition and Russia's invasion of Ukraine have opened new ownership options for the state offshore.

Norway is unlikely to end participation offshore. The government's April 2023 announcement that the state intends to nationalize the gas transit system when the current licenses expire (see Chapter 4) signaled new thinking among petroleum authorities. Nationalization of the gas network may be a one-off change to solve a major security headache. Or it may signal a broader move to extend participatory intervention with the state exercising its right to nationalize offshore production when licenses expire, which for many producing fields is before 2030 (NPD, 2023b). Why would the state take such a drastic step? Two realistic scenarios stand out. First, the security situation in the North Sea could deteriorate if tensions in Europe spill beyond the borders of Ukraine. The state may move to take ownership of offshore facilities if it believes that that is the only way to protect the infrastructure and production capacity. Second, a new government could take power in Norway having committed to transitioning fully and rapidly away from hydrocarbon production to storing CO_2 and producing hydrogen and wind-powered electricity. Nationalization to repurpose and decommission would resolve the tension Norwegians keenly feel between their commitment to extracting natural resources to benefit future generations (via the Oil Fund) and their almost religious devotion to nature and its preservation (Milne, 2023). Resolving that tension would raise many more questions as the economy and society adjust to the dismantling of an industry so many Norwegians working at home-grown companies rely on for their livelihoods. This embracing of Option 4 (Production Phase Out, Participatory Regime), while revolutionary, seems entirely possible in the Norwegian context. Perhaps such a change was foreshadowed by Statoil's name change to Equinor, which fits a company moving from producing fossil fuels to developing clean energy sources (Buljan, 2023).

British Conservative governments will not be nationalizing parts of the offshore sector. But a Labour government may well try to take control of a 'commanding height' or two. Labour leader Keir Starmer, in his 2022 conference speech, called for the creation of a new state-owned, 'clean generation company' called Great British Energy (GB Energy) to champion and develop sources of green energy. The proposed company, like the British National Oil

Corporation (BNOC) in the past, will work with the private sector to develop energy resources, but this time the company will focus on the 'sun, wind, and waves' to generate power (Labour, 2022). In the same speech, Starmer also called for the establishment of a sovereign wealth fund ('National Wealth Fund') to channel resources to British businesses. The party acknowledges that the time for a fund to collect petroleum profits has passed, but it is confident that other sources of revenue can be found (Labour, 2022). In short, Labour's interest in state participation in the energy sector, which lay dormant since the late 1980s, has re-emerged in the 2020s as a potential tool of energy policy.

Labour's participation agenda, like its pledge to end offshore petroleum licensing, is far from certain to pass Parliament. After taking power, campaign promises have a way of drifting to the bottom of the government's agenda as events rewrite priorities. For Labour to successfully enact its energy 'revolution', the party must first take power, and then it must put down a host of economic, political, and social interests certain to oppose the reimposition of state control over key elements of the energy sector. Green groups will also be watching. Already Starmer is getting pressure from environmental groups that want him to go farther, faster, and 'stop making U-turns' (Dawson, 2023).

EXPLAINING THE FUTURE

Britain and Norway are entering a new phase in the history of their offshore sectors. The energy transition has reached a tipping point: fossil fuels have peaked and are on the decline; alternative energy sources are on the rise. The continental shelves will continue to produce massive amounts of energy, but wind and hydrogen – and maybe waves and tides – will gradually replace declining oil and gas.

The North Sea system will not disappear. It will adapt to the new energy mix. States will control offshore activities through discretionary licensing systems, regulatory structures, taxation, and state participation. The whole offshore regulatory ecosystem will remain familiar to long-time North Sea observers. But two questions must be answered soon: what intervention regime will the two energy powerhouses adopt in the new world of mixed offshore energy? Regulatory? Participatory? And what petroleum strategy will Britain and Norway adopt? Maximum recovery? Wind down? The combination of answers to these questions informed our list of options described above (see Table 5.1).

Predicting the future, like explaining the past, entails examining the changes in system conditions, organized pressure, and political culture that encourage deeper state involvement offshore. System conditions will look similar for both countries. State capacity to regulate offshore energy activities will remain high. The North Sea oil and gas provinces will continue to decline, while prospects for bigger finds will remain in areas more distant from the shore, in deeper water, and in harsher climates. Oil prices will remain unpredictable, but may decline as western economies electrify or rise if Russian oil is withdrawn from the market. OPEC will not be particularly effective as a producer cartel, but sanctions on Russian hydrocarbons and a protracted land war in Europe will affect prices. Scarce petroleum will benefit Norway more than Britain. Securing vulnerable infrastructure, of course, will challenge the two governments if the War in Ukraine drags on or spills over.

Major changes in group pressures will influence offshore policy in both countries, but it remains unclear how the pressure will play out. Environmental groups are taking a more aggressive line against petroleum production as we saw above. The extent to which they can recruit public opinion and political parties to their cause is key to understanding the depletion policy each state will adopt. If the effects of climate change are obvious and painful, anti-oil groups and parties, particularly of the left, will gain control of government and force a decision to end petroleum activities, starting with a permanent ban on issuing new licenses and perhaps proceeding to the total shutdown of petroleum production. The method used to shut down production would depend on the ideology of the government in power. Right-wing governments, if forced to shut the industry down, would probably use a regulatory approach. Left-wing governments in Britain, Norway, and possibly an independent Scotland would be more likely to use a state-owned company – such as Petoro in Norway, or GB Energy in the UK – which could more easily compensate companies with state revenues from petroleum sales during the planned phase out of production. Norway would be more likely to use state participation to make the offshore transition to renewable energy sources, but as we have seen, the UK under Labour might also revive the public ownership tradition in Britain.

The offshore oil and gas companies will not submit to a dismantling of the offshore sector without a fight. And they will be persuasive. They will argue that the energy transition will be just that – a transition. Oil and gas will still be needed during the next decades as alternative sources are developed and the infrastructure is built (Mete, et al., 2020, p. 186). Perhaps the most likely outcome is a ban on frontier licenses, but a continuation of development in mature and maturing areas. No one will like the compromise: oil companies will chafe at the area restrictions and environmental groups will not like the continued drilling. Offshore companies, however, will still make money, and anti-oil groups will look forward to the repurposing of oil and gas infrastructure for carbon capture and green power production. No matter what strategies are adopted, the British and Norwegian states will have to take a leading role offshore – whether as participants or regulators – to meet the energy demands of a modern Europe while simultaneously preventing a planetary catastrophe.

References

Acorn. (2023). Growing our decarbonised future. Retrieved from https://www.theacornproject.uk.

Andal, Øystein. (2023, 10 January). The Norwegian petroleum tax system. *Norway's Tax Blog*. Retrieved from https://blogg.pwc.no/skattebloggen-en/the-norwegian-petroleum-tax-system.

Anderson, Owen L. and Christopher Kulander. (2015). The offshore petroleum licencing regime in the United States. In Tina Hunter (ed.), *Regulation of the Upstream Petroleum Sector: A Comparative Study of Licensing and Concession Systems.* Edward Elgar Publishing, 159–201.

Ausland, John C. (1979). *Norway, Oil, and Foreign Policy.* Westview Press.

Austvik, Ole Gunnar. (2009). *The Norwegian State as Oil and Gas Entrepreneur: The Impact of the EEA Agreement and EU Gas Market Liberalization.* VDM Verlag.

Badgamia, Nishtha. (2023, 30 June). Environmental groups sue Norwegian state, ask court to halt billion-dollar oil projects. *WION*. Retrieved from https://www.wionews.com/world/environmental-groups-sue-norwegian-state-ask-court-to-halt-recently-approved-billion-dollar-oil-projects-610304.

BAHR. (2022, 6 December). Offshore wind: Tender rules for Norway's first offshore wind licensing round. *Newsletter*. Retrieved from https://bahr.no/newsletter/offshore-wind-tender-rules-for-norways-first-offshore-wind-licensing-round.

Bektas, Cem, Marie Hubatova, and Aoife O'Leary. (nd). The Norwegian NOx Fund. *Environmental Defense Fund.* Retrieved from https://www.edf.org/search/content?keys=nox%20fund.

Beyond Oil and Gas Alliance (BOGA). (2023). Who we are. Retrieved from https://beyondoilandgasalliance.org/who-we-are/.

Birnie, Patricia W. (1975). The Legal Background to North Sea oil and gas development. In Martin Sæter and Ian Smart (eds.), *The Political Implications of North Sea Oil and Gas.* Universitetsforlaget.

Bjørnebye, Henrik and Catherine Banet. (2019). Licensing regime: Norway. In Eduardo G. Pereira and Henrik Bjørnebye (eds.), *Regulating Offshore Petroleum Resources.* Edward Elgar Publishing, 96–126.

Bridge, Gavin and Gisa Weszkalnys. (2023, 7 June). Keir Starmer hasn't really called time on North Sea oil and gas – here's why. *The Conversation.* Retrieved from https://theconversation.com/keir-starmer-hasnt-really-called-time-on-north-sea-oil-and-gas-heres-why-207091.

Brent crude oil. (2023). Trading Economics. Retrieved from https://tradingeconomics.com/commodity/brent-crude-oil.

Buli, Nora and Nerijus Adomaitis. (2022, 29 November). Norway delays 26th oil licensing round. *Offshore Engineer.* Retrieved from https://www.oedigital.com/news/501276-norway-delays-26th-oil-licensing-round.

Buljan, Adrijana. (2023, 5 January). Equinor, RWE unveil joint offshore wind-to-hydrogen plan for Norway and Germany. *OffshoreWIND.biz.* Retrieved from https://www

.offshorewind.biz/2023/01/05/equinor-rwe-unveil-joint-offshore-wind-to-hydrogen
-plan-for-norway-and-germany/.

Bunter, Michael. (2002). *The Promotion and Licencing of Petroleum Prospective Acreage*. Kluwer Law International.

BVG Associates. (2019, January). Guide to an offshore wind farm, updated and extended. Retrieved from https://www.thecrownestate.co.uk/media/2861/guide-to-offshore-wind-farm-2019.pdf.

Callow, Clive. (1973). *Power from the Sea: The Search for North Sea Oil and Gas*. Victor Gollancz.

Cameron, Peter D. (1983). *Property Rights and Sovereign Rights: The Case of North Sea Oil*. Academic Press.

Castberg, Johan. (1912, 12 August). Grundlinjen i vor politik – samfundssolidariteten. *Dagbladet*.

Cavcic, Melisa. (2022, 23 September). UK's first carbon storage licensing round brings 26 bids from 19 players. *Offshore Energy*. Retrieved from https://www.offshore-energy.biz/uks-first-carbon-storage-licensing-round-brings-26-bids-from-19-players/.

Center for Public Impact. (2019, 2 September). The Government Pension Fund Global (GPFG) in Norway. Retrieved from https://www.centreforpublicimpact.org/case-study/government-pension-fund-global-gpfg-norway.

Chapman, Keith. (1976). *North Sea Oil and Gas: A Geographical Perspective*. David and Charles.

Cocklin, Jamison. (2022, 17 March). Equinor cleared to keep Norwegian natural gas output near capacity to aid European supplies. *Natural Gas Intelligence*. Retrieved from https://www.naturalgasintel.com/equinor-cleared-to-keep-norwegian-natural-gas-output-near-capacity-to-aid-european-supplies/.

Colombia Center on Sustainable Investment. (2016). Local content: Norway – petroleum. Retrieved from https://ccsi.columbia.edu/sites/default/files/content/docs/Local%20Content%20-%20Norway%20Petroleum%20-%20CCSI%20-%20May%202016.pdf.

Corti, Gerry and Frank Frazer. (1983). *The Nation's Oil: A Story of Control*. Graham and Trotman.

Daintith, Terence. (2011). *Finders Keepers? How the Law of Capture Shaped the World Oil Industry*. Routledge.

Dam, Kenneth W. (1976). *Oil Resources: Who Gets What How?* University of Chicago Press.

Davis, Jerome. (2004, 18–21 March). *Does one size fit all? Reflecting on governance and North Sea licensing systems*. Background Paper: BC Offshore: Potential and Problems a MASC Workshop for Lawyers, Dunismuir Lodge, Sidney, BC.

Dawson, Bethany. (2023, 6 July). Keir Starmer's got 5 missions. Can the UK Labour boss accomplish them? *Politico.eu*. Retrieved from https://www.politico.eu/article/keir-starmers-five-missions-uk-labour-boss-accomplish/.

Department for Business, Energy and Industrial Strategy (BEIS). (2019, 25 February). Extractive industries in the UK: background information on oil and gas. Retrieved from https://www.gov.uk/government/publications/extractive-industries-transparency-initiative-payments-report-2017/extractive-industries-in-the-uk-background-information-on-oil-and-gas.

Dølvik, Jon Erik and Johannes Oldervoll. (2019). Norway: Averting crisis through coordination and Keynsian welfare policies. In Stefán Ólafsson, Mary Daly, Olli Kangas, and Joakim Palme, (eds.) *Welfare and the Great Recession: A Comparative Study*. Oxford Academic Press, 210–227.

Donaldson, Kitty. (2022, 7 September). Truss says she's against a UK windfall tax on energy companies. *Bloomberg.com*. Retrieved from https://www.bloomberg.com/news/articles/2022-09-07/truss-says-she-s-against-a-uk-windfall-tax-on-energy-companies#xj4y7vzkg.

Eder, Sascha. (2019, 22 May). Is Google the next Exxon? Why tech giants are after the oil and gas industry. *NewtonX*. Retrieved from https://www.newtonx.com/insights/2019/05/22/google-amazon-microsoft-oil-and-gas/.

Eide, Ole Jone. (nd-a). The road to the stock market. *Statoil and Equinor: The History of Norway's Most Valuable Company*. Retrieved from https://equinor.industriminne.no/en/the-road-to-the-stock-market/.

Eide, Ole Jone. (nd-b). Gassco – background, creation and function. *Statoil and Equinor: The History of Norway's Most Valuable Company*. Retrieved from https://equinor.industriminne.no/en/gassco-background-creation-and-function/.

Enoksen, Odd Roger. (2007, 22 March). Building a sustainable petroleum industry: The Norwegian experience. Speech given at Mexico-Norway Meeting on Cooperation in the Energy Sector. Retrieved from http://www.regjeringen.no/en/tidligere_statsraader/Minister-of-Petroleum-and-Energy/Speeches-and-articles/2007/Building-a-sustainable-petroleum-industr.html?id=460505.

Environmentalists sue Norway over new oil projects. (2023). *Yahoo! Finance*. Retrieved from https://finance.yahoo.com/news/environmentalists-sue-norway-over-oil-093533280.html.

European Parliament and of the Council. (1994, 30 May). Directive 94/22/EC on the conditions for granting and using authorizations for the prospection, exploration and production of hydrocarbons. *Official Journal of the European Communities,* No L 164/3. Retrieved from https://eur-lex.europa.eu/legal-content/EN/TXT/PDF/?uri=CELEX:31994L0022&from=DA.

European Council. (2023, 7 February). Infographic - where does the EU's gas come from? Retrieved from https://www.consilium.europa.eu/en/infographics/eu-gas-supply/.

Eurostat. (2023, 15 March). Oil and petroleum products – a statistical overview. Retrieved from https://ec.europa.eu/eurostat/statistics-explained/index.php?title=Oil_and_petroleum_products_-_a_statistical_overview&oldid=315177.

Financial Times European Energy Report. (1985, 22 March).

Forster, Malcolm, and Donald N. Zillman. (1983). The British National Oil Corporation: The state enterprise as an instrument of energy policy. *Energy Law and Policy,* 58. 57–111.

Fraser, Douglas. (2019, 6 October). A new monster from the deep. *BBC News*. Retrieved from https://www.bbc.com/news/uk-scotland-scotland-business-49954074.

Frewer, Geoff. (2004). Auctions vs. discretion in the licencing of oil and gas acreage. In G. MacKerron and Peter J. Pearson (eds.), *The International Energy Experience: Markets, Regulation, and the Environment*. Imperial College Press.

FuelCellsWorks. (2022, 14 December). Exclusive: North Sea body backs hydrogen hub to power 20m homes. *FuelCellsWorks*. Retrieved from https://fuelcellsworks.com/news/exclusive-north-sea-body-backs-hydrogen-hub-to-power-20m-homes/.

Gallafent, Kate, Jane Collier, and Rachel Jones. (2022, 19 January). R (Jeremy Cox and others) v (1) The Oil and Gas Authority, (2) Secretary of State for Business, Energy And Industrial Strategy [2022] EWHC 75 (Admin). *Blackstone Chambers*. Retrieved from https://www.blackstonechambers.com/news/r-jeremy-cox-and-others-v-1-the-oil-and-gas-authority-2-secretary-of-state-for-business-energy-and-industrial-strategy/.

Geiger, Julianne. (2023, 5 May). Norway's surprise natural gas nationalization plan even broader than expected. *OilPrice.com*. Retrieved from https://oilprice.com/ Latest-Energy-News/World-News/Norways-Surprise-Natural-Gas-Nationalization -Plan-Even-Broader-Than-Expected.html.

Gordon, Greg. (2011). Petroleum licencing. In Greg Gordon, John Paterson, and Emre Usenmez (eds.), *Oil and Gas Law: Current Practice and Emerging Trends*, 2nd edition. Dundee University Press, 65–110.

Gordon, Greg. (2019). Hydrocarbon policies and legislation: United Kingdom. In Eduardo G. Pereira and Henrik Bjørnebye (eds.), *Regulating Offshore Petroleum Resources*. Edward Elgar Publishing, 165–210.

Gormley, Tonje Pareli and Merete Kristensen. (2019). Hydrocarbon policy and legislation: Norway. In Eduardo G. Pereira and Henrik Bjørnebye (eds.), *Regulating Offshore Petroleum Resources*. Edward Elgar Publishing, 39–95.

Halpin, Danny. (2023, 29 March). Academics urge Sunak to end approvals for new oil and gas projects. *Evening Standard*. Retrieved from https://www.standard.co.uk/ news/politics/ipcc-ed-miliband-government-antonio-guterres-shetland-b1070622 .html.

Hamilton, Adrian. (1978). *North Sea Impact: Offshore Oil and the British Economy*. International Institute for Economic Research.

Helle, Egil. (1984). *Norges Olje—de Første 20 Årene*. Tiden Norsk Forlag.

HM Revenues and Customs. (2020). Statistics of Government revenues from UK Oil and Gas production. Retrieved from https://assets.publishing.service.gov.uk/government/ uploads/system/uploads/attachment_data/file/902798/Statistics_of_government _revenues_from_UK_oil_and_gas_production__July_2020_for_publication.pdf.

Hoopes, Stephanie M. (1984). *Oil Privatization, Public Choice and International Forces*. Palgrave McMillan.

Hunter, Tina. (2011). Sustainable socio-economic extraction of Australian offshore petroleum resources through legal regulation: Is it possible? *Journal of Energy & Natural Resources Law*, 29(2), 209–246.

Hunter, Tina. (2015). Granting access to petroleum resources under the licensing and concession system. In Tina Hunter (ed.), *Regulation of the Upstream Petroleum Sector: A Study of Licensing and Concession Systems*. Edward Elgar Publishing, 36–59.

International Energy Agency (IEA). (2020, 1 July). CO^2 tax on offshore oil and gas. Retrieved from https://www.iea.org/policies/11695-co2-tax-on-offshore-oil-and-gas.

Jacobsen, Alf R. (2010). *Snøhvit: The History of Oil and Gas in the Barents Sea*. Statoil.

Just Stop Oil: What is it and what does it want? (2023, 29 June). *BBC*. Retrieved from https://www.bbc.com/news/uk-63543307.

Keating, Cecilia. (2022, 19 January). High Court throws out legal challenge to UK's oil and gas production strategy. *BusinessGreen*. Retrieved from https://www.businessgreen .com/news/4043497/court-throws-legal-challenge-uk-oil-gas-production-strategy.

Keto, David B. (1978). *Law and Offshore Oil Development: The North Sea Experience*. Praeger.

Klapp, Merrie Gilbert. (1987). *The Sovereign Entrepreneur: Oil Policies in Advanced and Less Developed Capitalist Countries*. Cornell University Press.

Kongsnes, Ellen. (2004, 24 August). Ekofisk: Aging with pride. *DNV Managing Risk*. Retrieved from https://www.dropbox.com/home/B1%20%20North%20Sea%20Bk/ NORWAY%20by%20subject/Ekofisk%20REcovery?preview=ekofisk+ageing+ dnv.pdf.

KonKraft. (2023). Om oss. Retrieved from https://konkraft.no/main/om-oss/.

Kopp, Sandu-Daniel. (2015). *Politics, Markets and EU Gas Supply Security: Case Studies of the UK and Germany.* Springer.

Krogh, Finn E. (2023). Curbing the cash flow. *Statoil and Equinor: The History of Norway's Most Valuable Company.* Retrieved from https://equinor.industriminne.no/en/curbing-the-cash-flow/.

Kretzer, Ursula M. H. (1993). Overcapitalisation in licencing systems based on size of work programme, *Resources Policy,* 19(4), 299–311.

Kvendseth, Stig S. (1988). *Giant Discovery: A History of Ekofisk through the First 20 Years.* Phillips Petroleum Company Norway.

Labour. (2022, 27 September). Keir Starmer calls for new national champion in clean energy, Great British Energy, with a mission to cut bills, create jobs, and deliver energy independence. Retrieved from https://labour.org.uk/press/keir-starmer-calls-for-new-national-champion-in-clean-energy-great-british-energy-with-a-mission-to-cut-bills-create-jobs-and-deliver-energy-independence/.

Lawless, Jill. (2022, 7 September). UK leader Truss vows energy relief, rules out windfall tax. *AP News.* Retrieved from https://apnews.com/article/boris-johnson-biden-cabinet-liz-truss-d6d4a0e11edda9c70e84c77bdce75f20.

Lepic, Bojan. (2022, 30 November). Norway postpones 26th licensing round to 2025. *Rigzone.* Retrieved from https://www.rigzone.com/news/norway_postpones_26th_licensing_round_to_2025-30-nov-2022-171213-article/.

Lindroos, Maarit, Dominik Schnichels, and Lars Peter Svane. (2002, October). Liberalisation of European gas markets – Commission settles GFU case with Norwegian gas producers. Directorate-General Competition, European Commission, No. 3. Retrieved from https://ec.europa.eu/competition/publications/cpn/2002_3_50.pdf.

MacKay, D. I. and G. A. MacKay. (1975). *The Political Economy of North Sea Oil.* Martin Robertson.

McKie, Robin. (2021, 4 December). Environmental activists challenge 'unlawful' UK fossil fuel plan in high court. *The Guardian.* Retrieved from https://www.theguardian.com/environment/2021/dec/04/environmental-activists-challenge-unlawful-uk-fossil-fuel-plan-in-high-court.

Meredith, Sam. (2023). Norway faces backlash from campaigners for 'reckless' pursuit of Arctic oil and gas. *CNBC.com.* Retrieved from https://www.cnbc.com/2023/05/22/norway-urges-energy-giants-to-ramp-up-search-for-arctic-oil-and-gas.html.

Mete, Gokce, Wairimu Karanja, and Nduta Njenga. (2020). Fossil fuels and transitions: The UK maximising economic recovery strategy and low-carbon energy transitions. In Geoffrey Wood and Keith Baker (eds.), *The Palgrave Handbook of Managing Fossil Fuels and Energy Transitions.* Palgrave, 167–194.

Milne, Richard. (2023, 19 June). Norway will not 'shy away' from green transition dilemmas, says PM. *Financial Times.* Retrieved from https://www.ft.com/content/4f23b1d7-8b8b-4b1b-90cd-37c949e12117.

Ministry of Finance (Norway). (1974, 15 February). *Parliamentary Report No. 25 (1973–74) Petroleum Industry in Norwegian Society.* Unofficial English translation.

Ministry of Industry (Norway). (1971, 30 April). *Report No. 76 to the Norwegian Storting (1970–71) On the Exploration for and Exploitation of Submarine Natural Resources on the Norwegian Continental Shelf, etc.* Unofficial English translation.

Ministry of Industry (Norway). (1973, 2 February). *Storting Proposition No. 78 (1972–73) Exercise of the State's Option to Participate in the Petroleum Production License No. 024 (Frigg Field) and Assignment to Den Norske Stats Oljeselskap A/S*

(State Oil Company) of Agreements regarding State Participation in Production Licenses etc. Unofficial English translation.

Ministry of Petroleum and Energy (MPE). (2001–2002). *Report No. 38 to the Storting 2001–2: Oil and Gas Activities.* Unofficial English translation. Retrieved from https://www.regjeringen.no/contentassets/6e28af195e184f97940858665c2cebaa/sreportno38.pdf.

Ministry of Petroleum and Energy (MPE). (2004). *On the Petroleum Activity: Report No. 38 to the Storting.* Unofficial English translation. Retrieved from https://www.regjeringen.no/en/dokumenter/report-no-38-to-the-storting-2003-2004/id463802/.

Ministry of Petroleum and Energy (MPE). (2023, 21 March). Carbon capture and storage. Retrieved from https://www.norskpetroleum.no/en/environment-and-technology/carbon-capture-and-storage/#:~:text=Norway%20has%20extensive%20experience%20with,reinjected%20into%20sub%2Dseabed%20formations.

Ministry of Petroleum and Energy (MPE) and Ministry of Labour and Social Inclusion. (2022, 9 September). Guidelines for plan for development and operation of a petroleum deposit (PDO) and plan for installation and operation of facilities for transport and utilisation of petroleum (PIO). Retrieved from https://www.npd.no/globalassets/1-npd/regelverk/forskrifter/en/pdo-and-pio.pdf.

Morgan, Jon and Colin Robinson. (1976, May). A comparison of tax systems. *Petroleum Economist*, 170.

Muggeridge, A., A. Cockin, K. Webb, H. Frampton, I. Collins, T. Moulds, and P. Salino. (2014). Recovery rates, enhanced oil recovery and technological limits. *Philosophical Transactions of the Royal Society A* 372 (Online). Retrieved from http://rsta.royalsocietypublishing.org/content/roypta/372/2006/20120320.full.pdf.

Nasralla, Shadia. (2022, 18 January). Climate activists lose court case against UK oil regulator. *Reuters.* Retrieved from https://www.reuters.com/world/uk/climate-activists-lose-court-case-against-uk-oil-regulator-2022-01-18/.

Nelsen, Brent F. (1991). *The State Offshore: Petroleum, Politics, and State Intervention on the British and Norwegian Continental Shelves.* Praeger.

Nelsen, Brent F. (1992). Explaining petroleum policy in Britain and Norway, 1962–90. *Scandinavian Political Studies,* 15(4), 307–328.

Noreng, Øystein. (1979). Friends or Fellow Travelers? The Relation of Non-OPEC Exporters with OPEC. *Journal of Energy and Development,* 4(2), 326–327.

Noreng, Øystein. (1980). *The Oil Industry and Government Strategy in the North Sea.* Croom Helm.

Noreng, Øystein. (2004). The Norwegian experience of economic diversification in relation to petroleum industry. *Oil, Gas & Energy Law,* 4(2004), www.ogel.org.

North Sea Transition Authority (NSTA). (2022, 29 August). *Types of licence.* Retrieved from https://www.nstauthority.co.uk/licensing-consents/types-of-licence/.

North Sea Transition Authority (NSTA). (2023, 18 May). Huge net zero boost as 20 carbon storage licences offered for award. Press Release. Retrieved from https://www.nstauthority.co.uk/news-publications/news/2023/huge-net-zero-boost-as-20-carbon-storage-licences-offered-for-award/.

North Sea Transition Authority (NSTA). (2024). UKCS production. Retrieved https://www.nstauthority.co.uk/data-centre/nsta-open-data/production/.

Norwegian Petroleum. (2022). Production forecasts. Retrieved from https://www.norskpetroleum.no/en/production-and-exports/production-forecasts/#:~:text=In%202022%2C%20Norway%20produced%20232,somewhat%20lower%20than%20in%202021.

Norwegian Petroleum. (2023a). *Ekofisk.* Retrieved from https://www.norskpetroleum
.no/en/facts/field/ekofisk/.

Norwegian Petroleum. (2023b). The government's revenues. Retrieved from https://
www.norskpetroleum.no/en/economy/governments-revenues/#:~:text=The%20total
%20payment%20form%20tax,NOK%2077%20billion%20in%202023.

Norwegian Petroleum Directorate (NPD). (1996). *No. 72 Relating to Petroleum Activities*,
s 1–4. Retrieved from https://www.ilo.org/dyn/natlex/docs/ELECTRONIC/109390/
135689/F21296686/NOR109390.pdf.

Norwegian Petroleum Directorate (NPD). (2009, 29 January). Norwegian Petroleum
Directorate positive to APA. Retrieved from https://www.npd.no/en/news/general
-news/2009/Norwegian-Petroleum-Directorate-positive-to-APA/.

Norwegian Petroleum Directorate (NPD). (2018). Increasing oil and gas production in
the next five-year period. Retrieved from https://www.npd.no/en/facts/publications/
reports/the-shelf/the-shelf-in-2018/2-increasing-oil-and-gas-production-in-the-next
-five-year-period/.

Norwegian Petroleum Directorate (NPD). (2022a, 11 April). Licences for carbon storage.
Retrieved from https://www.npd.no/en/facts/carbon-storage/licences-for-carbon-storage/.

Norwegian Petroleum Directorate (NPD). (2022b, 12 July). Invitation to apply for petroleum
production licence. Retrieved from https://www.npd.no/en/facts/production-licences/
licensing-rounds/apa-2022/invitation-to-apply-for-petroleum-production-licence/.

Norwegian Petroleum Directorate (NPD). (2023a). *Factpages*. Retrieved from https://
factpages.npd.no/en/licence/pageview/all/27395665.

Norwegian Petroleum Directorate (NPD). (2023b). Production license, all-strategraphic
Factmaps. Retrieved from https://factmaps.npd.no/factmaps/3_0/.

Norwegian Petroleum Directorate (NPD). (2023c). Production forecasts. Retrieved from
https://www.norskpetroleum.no/en/production-and-exports/production-forecasts/.

Norwegian Petroleum Directorate (NPD). (2023d). Ormen Lange. Retrieved from
https://factpages.npd.no/en/field/PageView/All/2762452.

Norwegian Petroleum Directorate (NPD). (2023e). Ekofisk. Retrieved from https://
factpages.npd.no/en/field/pageview/all/43506.

Norwegian Tax Administration. (2023). NOx tax. Retrieved from https://www
.skatteetaten.no/en/business-and-organisation/vat-and-duties/excise-duties/about
-the-excise-duties/nox/.

Nyberg, Per Daniel, Jan Samuelsen, and Jonas Odland. (2022, 13 April). *Norway:
Revised proposal for a new petroleum tax system*. Retrieved from https://kpmg
.com/us/en/home/insights/2022/04/tnf-norway-revised-proposal-new-petroleum-tax
-system.html.

Offshore Norge. (2017). *Norway's Petroleum History.* Retrieved from https://offshorenorge
.no/en/about-us/oljehistorien/.

Parliamentary Energy Committee (Britain). (1985, 8 March). *Government Oil Price
Policy and the Spring Supplementary Estimate for £20 Million in Respect of the
British National Oil Corporation*, Session 1984–85.

Petoro. (nd). A driving force offshore Norway. Retrieved from https://www.petoro.no/
home.

Pickard, Jim and David Sheppard. (2023, 27 June). UK's projected windfall tax take
from North Sea levy drops 40%. *Financial Times.* Retrieved from https://www.ft
.com/content/8dfb1b63-5686-41db-899d-7965b6ec34f4.

Promote licenses bring new entrants to the North Sea. (2005, 11 November). *Offshore.*
Retrieved from https://www.offshore-mag.com/regional-reports/article/16764236/
promote-licenses-bring-new-entrants-to-the-north-sea.

Public Accounts Committee, Parliament (UK). (1973, February). *North Sea Oil and Gas [PAC Report]*, Session 1972–73.

Read, Stanley. (2023, 31 July). British government signals support for oil and gas industry. *The New York Times.* Retrieved from https://www.nytimes.com/2023/07/31/business/britain-drilling-north-sea.html.

Sampson, Anthony. (1975). *The Seven Sisters: The Great Oil Companies and the World They Shaped.* Bantam Books.

Sanders, Andreas R. D. (2023). *Democracy and Resource Nationalism: The Norwegian Concession Laws.* NTNU Case #14–2023.

Seely, Anthony. (2023, 25 April). Taxation of North Sea Oil and Gas. Research Briefing. House of Commons Library. Retrieved from https://researchbriefings.files.parliament.uk/documents/SN00341/SN00341.pdf.

Shackleton, Michael. (1978). Oil and the British foreign process. *Millennium: Journal of International Studies,* 7(2), 137–152.

Shell. (2023). *Ormen Lange.* Retrieved from https://www.shell.com/about-us/major-projects/ormen-lange.html.

Skopljak, Nadja. (2023, 18 May). 20 carbon storage licenses offshore UK offered to 12 companies. *Offshore Energy.* Retrieved from https://www.offshore-energy.biz/20-carbon-storage-licenses-offshore-uk-offered-to-12-companies/#:~:text=The%20NSTA%20launched%20the%20UK%27s,Teesside%2C%20Liverpool%2C%20and%20Lincolnshire.

Soliman Hunter, Tina. (2023). Development of regulatory regimes for offshore exploitation: The 'North American' and 'North Sea' Perspectives. In Tina Soliman Hunter and Madeline Taylor (eds.), *Research Handbook on Oil and Gas Law.* Edward Elgar Publishers, 65–88.

Storting. (1971, 14 June). *White Paper No. 76 (1970–1971) Exploration for and Exploitation of Subsea Natural Resources on the Norwegian Continental Shelf, etc.* Unofficial English translation.

Storting. (2011). *White Paper No. 28 (2010–2011) An Industry for the Future: Norway's Petroleum Activities.* Unofficial English translation.

Strange, Susan. (1988). *States and Markets,* 2nd edition. Pinter Publishers.

Sunnevåg, Kjell J. (2000). Designing auctions for offshore petroleum lease allocation. *Resources Policy,* 26(1), 3–16.

Taylor, Madeline and Tina Soliman Hunter. (2019). *Agricultural Land Use and Natural Gas Extraction Conflicts: A Global Socio-Legal Perspective.* Routledge.

Taylor, Matthew. (2023, 29 June). Campaigners vow to step up action against new North Sea oilfield. *The Guardian.* Retrieved from https://www.theguardian.com/uk-news/2023/jun/29/campaigners-vow-to-step-up-action-against-new-north-sea-oilfield.

Taverne, Bernard. (1999). *Petroleum Industry and Governments: An Introduction to Petroleum Regulation, Economics, and Government Policies.* Kluwer Law International.

Thomas, Allister. (2022, 18 January). Court throws out claim that government is 'unlawful' in supporting North Sea oil. *Energy Voice.* Retrieved from https://www.energyvoice.com/oilandgas/north-sea/380505/court-paid-to-pollute-north-sea-oil/.

Thompson, Helen. (2022). *Disorder: Hard Times in the 21st Century.* Oxford University Press.

Thurber, Mark C. and Benedicte Tangen Istad. (2010, 1 May). *Norway's Evolving Champion: Statoil and Politics of State Enterprise.* Working Paper. Program on Energy and Sustainable Development. Stanford University, Stanford.

Tomasgard, Asgeir and Goran Durakovic. (2023, 18 April). Yes, we should produce hydrogen in Norway. *Norwegian SciTech News.* Retrieved from https://norwegianscitechnews.com/2023/04/yes-we-should-produce-hydrogen-in-norway/.

Tønne, Tore. (1983). Energy policy: A Norwegian perspective. *Northwestern Journal of International Law and Business,* 5(4), 722–742.

Tonstad, Per Lars and Farouk Al-Kasim. (2023) *Our Oil – The Man and the Challenges.* Austin Macauley.

Troll A platform. (2022, 3 August). *Wikipedia.* Retrieved from https://en.wikipedia.org/wiki/Troll_A_platform.

Udgaard, Nils Morten. (1987). Norway between the IEA and OPEC: Oil prices and foreign policy. *The Offshore Digest,* 3, 27–28.

UK Offshore Energies Association (OEUK). (2022a, 15 November). There's enough oil & gas in North Sea to fuel UK for 30 years, but industry needs fiscal certainty. *Offshore Engineer.* Retrieved from https://www.oedigital.com/news/500942-oeuk-there-s-enough-oil-gas-in-north-sea-to-fuel-uk-for-30-years-but-industry-needs-fiscal-certainty.

UK Offshore Energies Association (OEUK). (2022b, 17 November). Chancellor's tax changes threaten long-term investment and consumers' energy security, warns. Offshore Energies UK. Press Release. Retrieved from https://oeuk.org.uk/chancellors-tax-changes/.

United Kingdom Government. (nd). The maximising economic recovery strategy for the UK. Presented to Parliament pursuant to Section 9(g) of the *Petroleum Act 1998* as amended by the *Infrastructure Act 2015.* Retrieved from https://assets.publishing.service.gov.uk/government/uploads/system/uploads/attachment_data/file/509000/MER_UK_Strategy_FINAL.pdf.

Vickers, John and Vincent Wright. (1989). *The Politics of Privatisation in Western Europe.* Routledge.

Walker, Peter. (2023, 28 May). Labour confirms plans to block all new North Sea oil and gas projects. *The Guardian.* Retrieved from https://www.theguardian.com/politics/2023/may/28/labour-confirms-plans-to-block-all-new-north-sea-oil-and-gas-projects.

Wallace, Abby. (2030, 31 July). Rishi Sunak to green-light hundreds of new oil and gas licenses in North Sea. *Politico.* Retrieved from https://www.politico.eu/article/rishi-sunak-oil-gas-licenses-north-sea/.

Williams, Trevor I. (1981). *A History of the British Gas Industry.* Oxford University Press.

Wood, Ian. (2014, 24 February). *UKCS Maximising Recovery Review: Final Report.* Retrieved from https://www.nstauthority.co.uk/media/1014/ukcs_maximising_recovery_review.pdf.

Index

predictable offshore tax system 94
pressure groups, divergence 71–2
'private ownership of minerals' 14
privatization 96–7
Production License 807 80
production licensees 18–19, 77, 85

reconnaissance licenses 21
reconvergence 74–9, 80–103
 Britain 100–3
 comparing systems 81–2
 depletion 86–92
  Britain 89–92
  Norway 86–9
 international context 74–7
 licensing 78–85
  Britain 78–9
  hydrocarbon directive, and
   82–5
  Norway 80–81
 Norway 100–3
 participation 96–9
 taxation 92–6
  Britain 92–4
  Norway 94–6
Reeves, Rachel 94
regulatory intervention 5
resource nationalism 20
responsibility 30
'ring fence' 42
 Corporation Tax (RFCT) 93
'rule of capture' 14
Russian domestic instability 105

Saga 38
Socialist Left (SV) party 81
sovereignty 16–17
Special Petroleum Tax (SPT) 95
'Special Tax' 41–2
Starmer, Keir 112–13
state bureaucracies 10
state capacity 105
state intervention 74, 104–105
state-owned petroleum company 27
state participation 71, 98, 112–13

State's Direct Financial Interest (SDFI)
 96
Statoil 38, 40–41, 96–8
Stewardship 90
Stoltenberg, Jens 97
Strange, Susan 1
strengthened tax system 33–4
substantial government ownership 44
Sunak, Rishi 82
Supplementary Charge (SC) 93–4
system conditions 8–9

taxation 41–2
tax neutrality 95
technical and financial capability 83
'Ten Oil Commandments' 28
Thatcher, Margaret 45
third-party access (TPA) 88
Third Round of licensing 38
Truss, Liz 94

UK Continental Shelf (UKCS) 18, 25,
 39, 74
UK Petroleum Act (1998) 84
UN Framework Convention on Climate
 Change (UNFCCC) 76
United Kingdom Offshore Operators
 Association (UKOOA) 34, 92–3
United Nations General Assembly
 Resolution 1803 83
'uplift' provision 42
Uplift UK 79
US petroleum exploitation 13

'Varley Assurances' 34
volatile petroleum prices 93

War in Ukraine 76, 105, 107, 114
Watercourse Concession Law 20
West Sole 23
Wilson, Harold 22, 34
Wood, Ian 90–91
World Snooker Championship 79
WWF-Norway 108